Boho Baby Crochet

First published in the UK in 2017 by
APPLE PRESS
74-77 White Lion Street
London N1 9PF
United Kingdom

www.quartoknows.com

ISBN: 978-1-84543-674-2

This book was conceived, designed and produced by Quantum Books Limited.
6 Blundell Street
London N7 9BH
United Kingdom

Publisher: Kerry Enzor
Managing Editor: Julia Shone
Editor: Charlotte Frost
Designer: Tokiko Morishima
Photographer: Simon Pask
Technical Consultant: Therese Chynoweth
Production Manager: Zarni Win

Printed in China by 1010 International Limited.
9 8 7 6 5 4 3 2 1

Disclaimer

The projects in this book have been designed with babies and toddlers in mind. Three dimensional pieces are crocheted seamlessly or securely fastened in place. Buttons, beads, sequins, and other plastic components have been avoided as often as possible. When making a project the authors and publisher urge the readers to ensure that all elements are securely joined and that there are no components that may become a choking hazard. Babies and toddlers should be supervised at all times when wearing, using, or playing with the projects contained in this book. Because there is always a risk involved, the author and publisher are not responsible for any adverse effects or consequences resulting from the making of any of the projects and please do not use this book if you are unwilling to assume the risk. The author and publisher expressly disclaim responsibility of any adverse effects arising from the use or application of the information contained in this book.

Boho Baby Crochet

30 Modern & Colourful Projects for Your Baby

Contributing Editor: Dedri Uys

APPLE PRESS

Contents

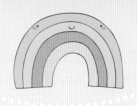

Introduction

I firmly believe that there is no greater gift for a baby than an item handmade with love. When I had my first son, a friend of ours made him a little octopus toy out of an old T-shirt. I cherished that toy right up until the day we lost it on an outing. There was something so comforting and special about the fact that she had taken the time to create a gift. It spoke of love and carried meaning.

This book is full of colourful projects for babies, each specially chosen for its vibrancy and texture. So whether you are looking for clothing, storage, or toys, you are sure to find something that says 'love' to both baby and baby's parents.

The patterns are rated from easy to advanced, and the techniques section covers everything you need to know to get started, beginning with how to hold your hook and ending with how to finish your projects.

I hope that you enjoy this book and that you find the perfect project for you!

Dedri

COLOURFUL CLOTHING

Rainbow Band Booties

The bright stripes on these booties will add a splash of colour to any outfit. Follow the stripe combination used in the pattern, or use shades of a single colour for an ombré effect.

YOU WILL NEED

Aran weight
50% merino/25% acrylic/
25% microfibre
(105 m/115 yd, 50 g/1.75 oz)

∗ 1 ball of beige (A)
Small amounts in the
following colours:
turquoise (B), bright green (C),
red (D), yellow (E), pink (F)

EQUIPMENT
∗ 4 mm (US G/6) crochet hook
∗ Tapestry needle

TENSION
17 sts and 13 rows = 10 cm (4") in
half treble crochet

SIZE
Size: 0–6 months
Ankle circumference: 13 cm (5")
Foot length from heel: 9 cm (3.5")

TO MAKE

Sole
Round 1: With A, work 9ch, 3tr into third ch from hook, 1tr in each of the next 5ch, 7tr into last ch turn work with opposite side of ch at top, 1tr in each of the next 5ch, 3tr in last ch, join with a sl st in top of 3ch at beg of round. (23 sts)

Round 2: 2ch, 2tr in each of next 3 sts, 1tr in next 5 sts, 2tr in each of the next 7 sts, 1tr in next 5 sts, 2tr into each of next 3 sts, join with a sl st in top of first tr. (36 sts) Break off yarn.

Upper
Round 1: Join A with a sl st in edge, 1ch, work BPhtr in each st around, join with a sl st in top of first BPhtr. (36 sts)

Round 2: 1ch, 1dc into in each st around, join with a sl st in top of first dc.

Round 3: 1ch, 1dc in first 10 sts, htr2tog 3 times, 1htr into next 4 sts, htr2tog 3 times, 1dc in next 10 sts, join with a sl st in top of first dc. (30 sts)

Round 4: 1ch, 1dc in next 8 sts, htr into next st, tr2tog 6 times, htr into next st, 1dc in next 8 sts, sl st in top of first dc. (24 sts)

Round 5: 1ch, 1dc in next 9 sts, dc2tog, ht2rtog, dc2tog, 1dc in next 9 sts, join with a sl st in top of first dc. (21 sts)

Leg

Rounds 6–10: 1ch, 1dc in each st to end, join with a sl st in top of first dc.

Break off yarn. Sew in all loose ends.

Stripes

Stripe 1: With B and RS facing, work a round of sl st between rounds 5 and 6. Break off yarn.

Stripe 2: With C and RS facing, work 1 round of sl st between rounds 6 and 7. Break off yarn.

Stripe 3: With E and RS facing, work 1 round of sl st between rounds 7 and 8. Break off yarn.

Stripe 4: With D and RS facing, work 1 round of sl st between rounds 8 and 9. Break off yarn.

Stripe 5: With F and RS facing, work 1 round of sl st between rounds 9 and 10. Break off yarn.

Stripe 6: With B and RS facng, work 1 round of sl st in top of round 10. Break off yarn.

FINISHING

Cut a strand of B. Thread strand under 2htrtog at centre at centre of round 5, then tie in a bow.

Sew in remaining ends.

Gumdrops Pullover

This lightweight sweater is perfect for blustery spring or autumn days. Made from an acrylic/cotton blend, it breathes well and is warm without being too heavy.

YOU WILL NEED

Aran weight
50% cotton/50% acrylic
(160 m/175 yd, 100 g/3.5 oz)

* 2 balls of baby blue (A)
* 1 ball in the following colours:
forest green (B), orange (C),
cobalt (D), gold (E), claret (F)

EQUIPMENT

* 5 mm (US H/8) crochet hook
* 4 mm (US G/6) crochet hook
* 3 locking stitch markers
* Tapestry needle

TENSION

13 sts and 8 rows = 10 cm (4") in
treble crochet with 5 mm (US H-8)

SIZE

Size: 6 months [12 months, 18 months]
Chest circumference: 53.5 [53.5,
56.5] cm (12 [21, 22¼]")
Length: 28 [30.5, 30.5] cm
(11 [12, 12]")
Shown in size 6 months.

TO MAKE

Gumdrop Stitch
(multiple of 3 sts + 2)

Round 1a (RS): Turn, sl st in first st, 1ch, place A on a removable stitch marker. Join next contrasting colour with sl st in next st, work 2ch (counts as tr), 1tr in next st, * 1ch, miss next st, 1tr in next 2 sts; repeat from * to end, 1ch keeping loop on st marker and working yarn at WS, join with a sl st in top of 2ch at beg of round, break off contrasting colour yarn.

Round 1b (RS): Return A to crochet

SPECIAL STITCHES

* BPtr (see page 114)
* FPtr (see page 114)
* Vst: 1tr, 1ch, 1tr in indicated stitch or space.

hook and pull it forward under the ch sp from round 1a; the working loop should now be in front, with yarn in back. Working over the chains from round 1a, work 3ch (counts as 1tr, 1ch, 1tr in same st, work Vst in each missed st of previous round, join with a sl st in second ch of 3ch at beg of round.

Round 2 (WS): 1ch, turn, 1htr in first 2tr from round 1a, * 1dc in next ch sp from round 1b, 1htr in next 2tr from round 1a; repeat from * to last ch sp from round 1b, dc in last ch sp, join with a sl st in top of first htr.
Repeat rounds 1a–2 for pattern.

Cuffs (make 2)

Foundation ch: With A and smaller crochet hook, loosely work 18 ch, join with a sl st in first ch to form a ring, being careful not to twist chain.

Round 1 (RS): 3ch (counts as 1tr), 1tr in back bar of next ch and each ch around, join with a sl st in top of 3ch at beg of round.

Round 2: 2ch (counts as BPtr), *FPtr around next st, BPtr around next st; repeat from * to last st, FPtr around last st, join with a sl st in top of 2ch at beg of round.

Repeat last round 1 more time.

Change to larger crochet hook.

Next round (WS): 1ch, turn, 1dc in each st to end, join with sl st in top of first dc. Do not break off yarn.

Arms (make 2)

Continuing from cuffs.

Rounds 1a and 1b (RS): With B, work rounds 1a and 1b of Gumdrop St.

Round 2 (WS): 1ch, turn, 1htr in first tr, 1htr in next tr, repeat from * in round 2 of Gumdrop Stitch Pattern, up to last 2tr from round 1a, 1htr in next tr, 2tr in next tr, 1dc in last ch sp, join with a sl st in top of first htr.

Round 3a (RS): Turn, sl st in first st, place A on removable st marker, miss next st, join C with a sl st in next st, 2ch (counts as 1tr), dc in next st, repeat from * in round 1a of Gumdrop

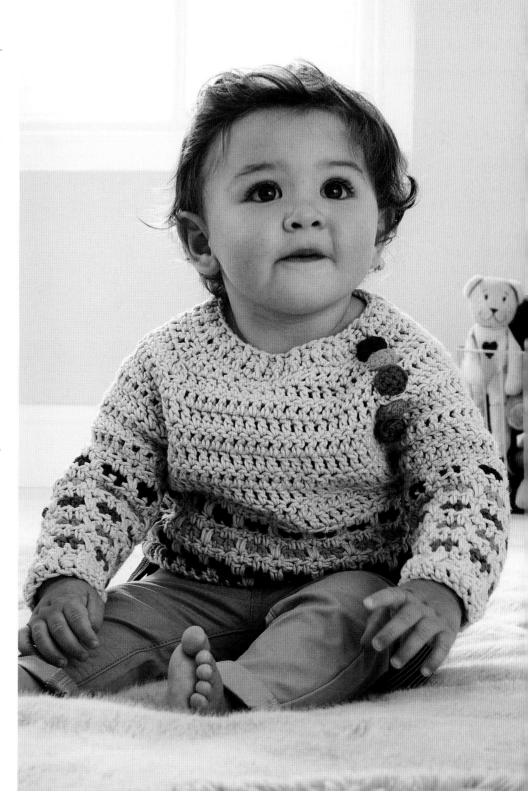

keeping A at WS, join D with a sl st in top of 2ch at beg of round. Break off.

Round 5b (RS): Return A to hook and pull it forward under the ch sp from round 5a; 2ch (counts as 1tr), 1Vst in each remaining missed st from previous round, join with a sl st in second ch of 2ch at beg of round.

Round 6 (WS): 1ch, turn, 1htr in next tr from round 5a, *1dc in next ch sp from round 5b, 1htr in next 2tr from round 5a; repeat from * to last ch sp, 1dc in next ch sp from round 5b, 1htr in next tr from round 5a, 1dc in last st from round 5b, join with a sl st in top of first 1htr.

Round 7a (RS): Turn, sl st in first st, 1ch, place A on removable st marker, join E with a sl st in next st, 2ch (counts as 1tr), 1tr in same st, * 1ch, miss next st, 1tr in next 2 sts; repeat from * to last 2 sts, 1ch, miss next st, 2tr in next st, 1ch, keeping A and working yarn from previous round at WS, join with a sl st in top of 2ch at beg of round. Break off E.

Round 7b (RS): Work round 1b of established pattern.

Round 8 (WS): Work round 2 of established pattern. (24 sts)

Round 9a (RS): With F, work round 1a of established pattern.

Round 9b (RS): Work round 1b of established pattern.

Round 10 (WS): Working into 1tr

st to last st, miss last st, do not join, break off B.

Round 3b (RS): Pick up A, 3ch, 2tr in next st, 1Vst in each missed st from previous round up to last missed st, 2tr in last missed st, join with sl st into 3ch at beg of round.

Round 4 (WS): 1ch, 1dc in first 2 sts, * 1htr in next 2tr from round 3a, 1dc in next ch sp from round 3b; repeat from * 4 more times, 1htr in next 2tr from round 3a, 1dc in last 3tr from round 4b, join with sl st into 1ch at beg of round.

Round 5a (RS): Turn, sl st in first st, 1ch, place A on removable st marker, join D with a sl st in next st, 2ch (counts as 1tr), * 1ch, miss next st, 1tr in next 2 sts; rep from * to last 2 sts, 1ch, miss next st, tr in next st, 1ch, from round 9a, and ch sp from round 9b, 1ch, turn, 2htr in first tr, 1htr in next tr * 1dc in next ch sp, 1htr in next 2tr; repeat from * to last ch2sp, 1dc in next ch sp, 1htr in next tr, 2htr in next tr, 1dc in last ch sp, join with a sl st in top of first 1htr. (26 sts)

Sizes 6 months only

Round 11: Turn, sl st in first st, 1ch, 1dc in each st to end, join with a sl st in top of first 1dc. (26 sts)

Size 12 months only

Round 11: Turn, sl st in first st, 1ch, 1dc in each st to last st, 1dc in last st, join with sl st in 1ch at beg of round. (26 sts)

Round 12: Turn, sl st in first st, 3ch (counts as 1tr), 1tr in each st up to last st, 2 tr in last st, join with a sl st in top of 3ch at beg of round. (27 sts)

Sizes 18 months only

Round 11: Turn, sl st in first st, 3ch (counts as tr), 1tr in each st up to last st, 2tr in last st, join with sl st in 3ch at beg of round. (27 sts)

Round 12: 3ch (counts as tr), turn, 1tr in each st to last st, 2tr in last st, join with a sl st in top of 3ch at beg of round.
   Repeat last round once (29 sts).

All sizes

Next round: Turn, sl st in first st, 3ch (counts as tr), 1tr in each st to end, join with a sl st in top of 3ch at beg of round.
   Repeat last round 0 [1, 0] more time(s). Break off at end of last round. Work should measure approximately 12.5 [15, 16] cm (5 [6, 6¼]") from beg.
   Turn work, miss first st, place marker in next st. Set aside.

Body

Foundation ch: With A and smaller crochet hook, loosely work 72 [72, 74] ch. Do not join.

Row 1 (RS): Beg in fourth ch from hook, 1tr in back bar only of each ch to end, join with a sl st in top of 3ch at beg of row, being careful not to twist. (70 [70, 72] sts)

Round 2: 2ch (counts as BPtr), *FPtr around next st, BPtr around next st; rep from * up to last st, FPtr around last st, join with a sl st in top of 2ch at beg of round.
   Change to larger crochet hook.

Size 18 months only

Next round: 1ch, turn, 1dc in each st to end, join with a sl st in top of first 1dc.

Sizes 6 months [12 months] only

Next round: 1ch, turn, 1dc in each st up to last 2 sts, dc2tog, join with a sl st in top of first dc. (69 sts)

All sizes

Working in Gumdrop st, work rounds 1a–2 five times, working contrasting colours as follows: B, C, D, E, then F.

Sizes 6 months only

Next round: Turn, sl st in first st, 3ch (counts as tr), 1tr in next st and in each st to last 2 sts, tr2tog, join with a sl st in top of 3ch at beg of round. (68 sts)

Size 12 months only

Next round: 1ch, turn, dc2tog, 1dc in each st to end, join with a sl st in top of dc2tog. (68 sts)

Size 18 months only

Next round: 1ch, turn, 1dc in next st and each st to end. (72 sts)

All sizes

Next round: Turn, sl st in first st, 3ch (counts as tr), 1tr in each st to end.
   Repeat last round 0 [2, 2] more times. Work should measure approximately 14 [16.5, 16.5] cm (5½ [6½, 6½]") from beg.

Yoke

Joining round: With RS of body facing, sl st in first 2 sts, 2ch (does not count as tr), miss st at base of ch, 1tr in next 29 [29, 31] sts, tr2tog, place marker in last st made, with RS of sleeve facing, tr2tog in marked st and next st on sleeve, remove marker, tr in next 20 [21, 23] sts, tr2tog, place marker in last st made, leaving remaining sleeve sts unworked, continue along body, miss next 2 sts, tr2tog, 1tr in next 28 [28, 30] sts, tr2tog, place marker in last st, with RS of remaining sleeve facing, tr2tog in marked st and next st, 1tr in next 20 [21, 23] sts, tr2tog, leave remaining 2 sleeve sts and 1 body st(s) unworked, join with a sl st to first 1tr on body. (104 [106, 114] sts; 30 [30, 32] sts each for front and back, and 22 [23, 25] sts for each sleeve).

Decrease round: Turn, sl st in first st, 2ch (does not count as st), miss first st, *1tr in each st to 2 sts before marker, tr2tog, move marker to dec st, tr2tog; rep from * twice more, 1tr up to last 2 sts, tr2tog, join with a sl st in top of first 1tr. (96 [98, 106] sts)

Repeat decrease round 5 [5, 6] more times. (56 [58, 58] sts; 18 sts each for front and back, and 10 [11, 11] sts for each sleeve).

Shape Front Neck

Sizes 6 months [12 months] only

Next round: Turn, sl st in first st, 2ch (does not count as a st), miss first tr, *1tr in each st to 2 sts before marker, tr2tog, remove marker, tr2tog**, 1tr in next 3 sts, htr in next 3 sts, 1dc in next 2 sts, htr in next 3 sts, 1tr in next 3 sts, tr2tog, remove marker, tr2tog; repeat from * to **, 1tr in each st to last 2 sts, join with a sl st in first tr. (48 [50] sts)

Size 18 months only

Decrease round: Turn, sl st in first st, 2ch (does not count as a st), miss first 1tr, *1tr in each st to 2 sts before marker, tr2tog, remove marker, tr2tog; repeat from * once more, 1tr in next 3 sts, htr in next 3 sts, 1dc in next 2 sts, htr in next 3 sts, 1tr in next 3 sts, tr2tog, remove marker, tr2tog, tr in each st to last 2 sts, tr2tog, join with a sl st in first 1tr. (50 sts).

All sizes

Change to smaller crochet hook.

Round 1 (WS): Turn, sl st in first st, 3ch (counts as tr), 1tr in each st around, join with a sl st in top of 3ch at beg of round.

Round 2 (RS): Turn, sl st in first st, 2ch (counts as BPtr), *FPtr around next st, BPtr around next st; repeat from * to last st, FPtr around last st, join with a sl st in top of 2ch at beg of round.

FINISHING

Sew in ends. Block to measurements (see page 121). Sew underarm seams.

(see page 121)

Buttons (make 5)

Round 1 (WS): With smaller crochet hook and B, 2ch, 6dc in second ch from hook, join with a sl st in first dc. (6 sts)

Round 2 (RS): Turn, 1ch, 1dc in first st, *1ch, 1dc in next st; repeat from * to end. Break off with an invisible join, leaving a long tail for sewing.

Make 4 more buttons, 1 each with colours C, D, E, and F.

Sew buttons securely to left front yoke along raglan line (this is the diagonal line that joins the sleeve to the rest of the pullover. Use photo as a guide), using running st or back st along edges.

Ombré Socks

These ombré socks are a modern take on traditional white socks. They are great for using up leftover yarns and turning them into something pretty and functional!

YOU WILL NEED

4 ply weight
55% wool/33% microfibre/
12% cashmere
(125 m/137 yd, 50 g/ 1.75 oz)

1 ball in the following colours:
* **Blue socks:** white (A),
baby blue (B), sky blue (C),
and electric blue (D)
* **Yellow socks:** white (A),
pale yellow (B), gold (C),
bright yellow (D)

EQUIPMENT
* 3.5 mm (US E/4) crochet hook
* Stitch markers
* Tapestry needle

TENSION
24 sts and 24 rounds = 10 cm (4")
in double crochet

SIZE

Size: 6–12 months [1–3 years]
Foot circumference: 5.5 [14] cm
(4 [10½]")
Foot length from heel:
10 [13]cm (4 [5]")

TO MAKE

Cuff

Foundation ch: With A, work 11ch.
Row 1 (RS): Beg in second ch from hook, 1dc into each ch to end, 1ch, turn. (10 sts)
Row 2 (WS): 1ch (doesn't count as dc) 1dc in back loop only to end, 1ch turn. (10 sts)
Rows 3–26 [30]: Repeat row 2. Mark last stitch of last row. Work should measure approximately 3.75 [4.5] cm (1½ [1¾]").
Joining row: Holding both short ends together, *sl st in 1ch at beg of row and front loop only of last row; repeat from * to end. Break off.

Ankle

Round 1: Join yarn B with a sl st in marked last st of cuff, 1dc in same st, 1dc in each row to end, join with a sl st in first dc. (26 [30] sts)
Round 2: 1ch (does not count as dc), 1dc in first st, 1ch, miss next st, * 1dc in next st, 1ch, miss next st; repeat from * 11 [13] more times, join with a sl st in first dc.
Round 3: 2ch, miss first ch sp, * 1dc in next ch sp, 1ch, miss next st; repeat from * 11 [13] more times, 1dc in last ch sp join with a sl st in first ch at beg of round.
Round 4: 1ch, * 1dc in next ch sp, 1ch, miss next st; repeat from * 12 [14] more times, join with a sl st in beg-ch.
Rounds 5–7: Repeat rounds 3–5.
Round 8: Repeat round 4. Break off.

Foot

Round 9: Join C with a sl st in ch sp

after join of last round, *dc in same ch sp, 1ch, miss next st; repeat from * 5 [6] more times, 1dc in next ch sp, ch 13 [15], miss 13 [15] sts, join with a sl st in first dc.

Round 10: 2ch, * 1dc in 1chsp, 1ch, miss next st; repeat from * 5 [6] more times, (1dc in ch, 1ch, miss next ch) 6 [7] times, dc in last ch, join with a sl st in first ch.

Repeat rounds 4 and 5 two [three] times. Break off yarn.

Next round: Join yarn D with a sl st into ch sp after join of last round; repeat round 2.

Next round: Repeat round 3.

Repeat rounds 4 and 5 twice.

Toe

Note: Work the toe in a spiral without joining at the end of each round.

Next row: 1ch (does not count as dc), dc in each st to end, do not join.

Size 6–12 months only

Decrease round 1: Dc2tog, *2dc, dc2tog; repeat from * 5 more times. (19 sts)

Decrease round 2: 1dc, *1dc into next st, dc2tog; repeat from * 5 more times. (13 sts)

Decrease round 3: 1dc, *dc2tog; repeat from * 5 more times. (7 sts)

Size 1–3 years only

Decrease round 1: *3dc, dc2tog; repeat from * 5 more times. (24 sts)

Decrease round 2: *2dc, dc2tog; repeat from * 5 more times. (18 sts)

Decrease round 3: *1dc, dc2tog; repeat from * 5 more times. (12 sts)

Decrease round 4: *Dc2tog; repeat from * 5 more times. (6 sts)

All sizes

Break off yarn. Thread tail through top of remaining sts and pull to close hole.

Heel

Round 1: Join A into any of the heel sts, 1ch, work 26 (30) dc around heel, join with sl st in top of first dc. (26 [30] sts)

Round 2: 1ch (does not count as dc), 1dc in next 2 sts, *dc2tog, 4 [5] dc; repeat from * 3 more times, join with a sl st in first dc. (22 [26] sts)

Round 3: 1ch (does not count as dc), 1dc in next 2 sts, *dc2tog, 3 [4] dc; repeat from * 3 more times, join with a sl st in first dc. (18 [22] sts)

Round 4: 1ch (does not count as dc), 1dc in next 2 sts, *dc2tog, 2 [3] dc; repeat from * 3 more times, join with a sl st in first dc. (14 [18] sts)

Size 1–3 years only

Round 5: Ch 1 (does not count as dc), sc in next 2 sts, *dc2tog, 2dc; repeat from * 3 more times, join with a sl st in first sc. (14 sts)

All sizes

Break off, leaving a long tail for seam.

FINISHING

Fold heel with 7 sts on each side, and folds at sides of heel. Use long tail to sew sts together. Break off yarn. Sew in loose ends.

STASH BUSTING
WITH SOCKS

These cute socks are the perfect way to use up small amounts of yarn in your stash. Any 4 ply-DK-weight yarn can be used with the same tension and patterns. The 4-ply weight yarn will produce socks with a lighter fabric. So why not look at your stash and explore the world of colour?

SAFETY FIRST

Beads can be a choking hazard for
small children. If you decide to sew
beads to this playsuit, make sure to
securely attach them. Do not leave
the baby unattended.

Little Flowers Playsuit

This dainty and elegant playsuit is the perfect project for newborn and milestone photos with your favourite professional photographer.

YOU WILL NEED

Lace weight
77% alpaca/23% silk
(140 m/153 yd, 25 g/0.88 oz)

* 1 [2] ball of off white
* Small amounts of lace weight yarn, 4 colours of choice for flowers

EQUIPMENT

* 5 mm (US H/8) crochet hook
* 4 mm (US G/6) crochet hook
* 3.25 mm (US D/3) crochet hook
* Tapestry needle
* 4 small beads (optional)

TENSION

15 sts and 10 rows = 10 cm (4") in half treble crochet

SIZE

Size: Newborn [6 months]
Hip circumference: 30 [33.5] cm (11¾ [13¼]")
Length, including edgings: approximately 40.5 [50] cm (16 [19¾]")
Shown in size Newborn.

TO MAKE

Foundation ch: With largest crochet hook and main colour yarn, work 44 [50]ch, join with a sl st into first ch. Do not twist.

Round 1: Ch 1 (does not count as htr), 1htr in each st to end, join with a sl st in first htr.

Repeat round 1 until work measures 20.5 [26] cm, (8 [10¼]") from beg.

Legs

Round 1: 1ch (does not count as htr), work 1htr in next 22 [25]sts, join with sl st in first htr, leaving remaining sts unworked for second leg. (22 [25] sts)

Round 2: 1ch (does not count as htr), htr in each st around, join with a sl st in first htr.

Repeat round 2 until leg measures 16.5 [20.5] cm, (6½ [8]").

Leg Edging

Size Newborn only

Next round: 1ch, miss next st, slst into next st, * miss next st, 5tr in next st, miss next st, sl st in next st; repeat from * 3 more times, miss next st, 5tr in next st, miss 2sts, sl st in first sl st of round.(5 shells) Break off yarn.

Size 6 months only

Next round: 2ch (counts as tr), 2tr in same st, * miss next st, sl st in next st, miss next st, 5tr in next st; repeat from * 4 more times, miss next st, sl st in next st, miss 2sts, 2tr in base of ch at beg of round, join with a sl st in top ch at beg of round. [6 shells] Break off.

(12 shells) Break off yarn.

Both sizes

Ties (make 4)

With size 4 mm (US G/6) crochet hook and main yarn, join yarn to foundation ch 3 [4] cm (1¼ [1½]") from side edge behind top edging, ch 50 [55].
Break yarn off.

Make 3 more ties, with 2 on front and back, and on each side of trousers.

FINISHING

Sew in ends.

Flowers (make 4)

With smallest crochet hook and colour of choice, make a magic ring.

Round 1: 1ch, 10dc in ring, pull tail to tighten ring, join with a sl st into top of first dc. (10 sts)

Round 2: 1ch, sl st in same st, 5tr in next st, * sl st in next st, 5tr in next st; repeat from * 3 more times, join with a sl st in first sl st. (5 petals)

Break off yarn, leaving a long tail.

Using tails, sew flowers to playsuit evenly spacing flowers across front. If using, sew beads to centre of flowers.

Sew in remaining ends.

Both sizes

Second Leg

With largest crochet hook, join main yarn in next st after first leg with a sl st.

Round 1: 1ch (does not count as htr), work 1htr in next 22 [25]sts. (22 [25] htr)

Repeat round 1 until left measures 16.5 [20.5] cm (6½ [8]").

Work edging in same way as first leg. Break off yarn.

Top Edging

With largest crochet hook, join main yarn on side edge of foundation ch.

Size Newborn only

Next round: 2ch (counts as tr), 2tr into same st, * miss next st, sl st in next st, miss next st, 5tr in next st repeat from * 9 more times, miss next st, sl st in next st, miss next st, 2tr in base of ch at beg of round, join with sl st in top of ch at beg of round. (11 shells) Break off yarn.

Size 6 months only

Next round: 1ch, sl st into same st and in next st, * miss next st, sl st in next st, miss next st, 5tr in next st; repeat from * 10 more times, miss next st, sl st in next st, miss next st, 2tr in base of ch at beg of round, join with sl st in top of ch at beg of round.

Rainbow Striped Cardigan

The stylish asymmetric front band and bright rainbow cuffs add a fun twist to this classic cardigan design.

YOU WILL NEED

DK weight
60% cotton/40% acrylic
(140 m/153 yd, 50 g/1.75 oz)

* 3 balls of white (A)
* 1 ball in the following colours:
red (B), yellow (C), grass green
(D), cobalt (E), purple (F)

EQUIPMENT
* 4 mm (US G/6) crochet hook
* Removable stitch marker or
safety pin
* Tapestry needle
* Four 15 mm (¾") buttons

TENSION
16 sts and 13 rows = 10 cm (4") in
half treble crochet

SIZE
Size: 3–6 months [6–12 months]
Chest circumference: 51 [56] cm
(20 [22]")
Length: 26 [29] cm (10¼ [11½]")
Shown in size 6–12 months.

TO MAKE

Back
Foundation ch: With yarn A work 41
[45]ch.
Row 1 (RS): Beg in third ch from hook
(counts as htr), 1htr in the back bump
only of each ch to end, turn.
(40 [44] sts)
Row 2: 2ch (counts as htr), 1htr in
each st to end, turn.
　Repeat row 2 until work measures
16.5 [18] cm (6½ [7]") from beg,
ending with a RS row.

Armholes
Next row (WS): 1ch, sl st in next
4 [6] sts, 2ch (counts as htr), 1htr in
each st up to last 4 [6] sts, turn. (32 sts)
Next row: 2ch (counts as 1htr), 1htr
in each st to end, turn.
　Repeat last row until armholes
measure 7 [8.25] cm (2¾ [3¼]").

Shape Neck
Next row: 2ch (counts as htr), 1htr in
next 8 sts, sl st in next 14 sts, 1htr in
each st to end, turn. (9 sts remain for
each shoulder – do not count sl sts).
Next row: 2ch (counts as htr), 1htr
into next 8 sts, sl st into next 14 sts, 1htr
into each st to end, turn. Break off yarn,
leaving a long tail to sew. Back measures
26.5 [29.25] cm (10.5" [11.5"]).

Sleeves (make 2)
Foundation ch: With A work 25 [27]ch.
Row 1 (RS): Beg in third ch from

hook (2ch counts as htr), htr in the back bump of each ch to end, turn. Break off yarn but do not turn. (24 [26] sts)

Row 2 (RS): With RS facing, join F with a sl st in top of ch at beg of row, 2ch (counts as htr), 1htr in back bar only of each st to end. Break off yarn, leaving a long tail for sewing. Do not turn.

Row 3 (RS): Join E and repeat row 2.

Row 4 (RS): With RS facing, join D with a sl st in top of 2ch from beg of prev row, (2ch (counts as htr) work an additional htr in top of 2ch from beg of prev row, working in the back bar only, work htr to end. Break off yarn, leaving a long tail for sewing. (25 [27] sts)

Row 5 (RS): With RS facing, join C with sl st in top of ch at beg of row, 2ch (counts as htr), work 1htr in back bar of each st up to last st, 2htr into last st. Break off yarn leaving a long tail for sewing. (26 [28] sts)

Row 6 (RS): Join B and repeat row 2.

Row 7 (RS): Join A and repeat row 4, but do not break off yarn at end of row, turn. (27 [29] sts)

Row 8 (WS): 2ch (counts as htr), 1htr in base of ch at beg of row, 1htr into each st to end, turn. (28 [30] sts)

Repeat row 8 four [six] more times. (32 [36] sts)

Keep working rows of 1htr into each st until work measures 15 [17] cm (6 [6¾]") from beg. Break off yarn, leaving a long tail for sewing.

Left Front

Foundation ch: With A, work 19ch.

Row 1 (RS): Beg in third ch from hook (counts as htr), 1htr in the back bump of each ch to end, turn. (18 [22] sts)

Row 2: 2ch (counts as htr), 1htr in each st to end, turn.

Repeat row 2 until work measures 16.5 [18] cm (6½ [7]") from beg, ending with a RS row.

Armhole

Next row (WS): 2ch (counts as htr), 1htr in each st to last 4 [6] sts, turn. (14 [12] sts)

Next row: 2ch (counts as htr), 1htr in each st to end, turn.

Repeat last row until armhole measures 7 [8.25] cm (2¾ [3¼]"), ending with a WS row.

Shape Neck

Next row (RS): 2ch (counts as htr), 1htr in each st, to last 9 [5] sts, turn. (5 [7] sts remain for shoulder—do not count sl sts).

Next row (WS): 2ch (counts as htr), 1htr in each st to end, turn.

Repeat last row until armhole measures 10 [11.5] cm (4 [4½]"). Break off yarn, leaving a long tail. Left front measures 26.5 [29.25] cm (10.5" [11.5"]).

Right Front

Foundation ch: With A, work 19 [23] ch.

Row 1 (RS): Beg in third ch from hook (counts as htr), 1htr in the back bump of each ch to end, turn. (18 [22] sts)

Row 2: 2ch (counts as htr), 1htr in each st to end, turn.

Repeat row 2 until work measures 16.5 [18] cm (6½ [7]") from beg, ending with a RS row.

Armhole

Next row (WS): 1ch, sl st in each of the next 4 [6] sts, 2ch (counts as htr), 1htr in each st to end, turn. (14 [16] sts)

Next row: 2ch (counts as htr), 1htr in each st to end, turn.

Repeat last row until armhole measures 7 [8.25] cm (2¾ [3¼]"), ending with a RS row.

Shape Neck

Next row: 1ch, sl st in next 9 sts, 2ch (counts as htr), 1htr in each st to end, turn. (5 [7] sts remain for shoulder—do not count sl sts).

Next row: 2ch (counts as htr), 1htr in each st to end, turn.

Repeat last row until armhole measures 10 [11.5] cm (4 [4½]"). Break off yarn, leaving a long tail. Right front measures 26.5 [29.25] cm (10.5" [11.5"]).

FINISHING

Sew in ends. Block pieces to measurements (see page 121)

With right sides facing, sew back and fronts together at shoulders.

Sew in sleeves along vertical and sl st edges of armholes.

Sew side and sleeve seams, using tails of stripe colours at cuffs to sew those sections together.

Rainbow Band

Row 1 (RS): With RS facing, join A with a sl st at bottom of right front, 1ch, 1dc in same st, work 35 [39] more dc evenly spaced along right front edge to neck. Fasten off. (36 [40] sts)

Row 2 (RS): Join F with a sl st in first sc of previous row, 2ch, (counts as htr), 1htr in each st to end. Break off yarn.

Row 3 (RS): Join E with a sl st in first htr of previous row, 2ch (counts as htr), 1htr in back bar of each st to end. Break off yarn.

Row 4 (RS): Join D and repeat row 3.

Row 5 (RS): Join C and repeat row 3.

Row 6 (RS): Join B and repeat row 3.

Buttonhole row (RS): Join A, 2ch (counts as htr), miss next st, working in the back bar of each st, htr in next 11 [12] sts, 1ch, miss next st, 1htr in next 10 [12] sts, 1ch, miss next st, 1htr in 10 [11] sts, 1ch, 1htr in last st in last st, place removable marker or safety pin in loop.

Sew in ends of rainbow band.

Front, Neck, and Bottom Edging

Return loop to crochet hook. Note: work this final edging row through both the front and back loops of each stitch along horizontal edges.

With RS facing and working along neck edge, work 1htr in space between each colour row, continue around neck edge, 1dc in each sl st or missed st, 1dc in each row along vertical neck edges, work 2dc in corner st, dc down left front edge, 2dc in corner st, 1dc in each st of foundation ch and 1dc in space between each colour row, work (1htr, 2dc) in ch at beg of last row of rainbow band, work 2dc in each ch sp and 1dc in each st along right front, then 1dc in last htr of row, continue across end of rainbow band, dc to end of rainbow band, then join using invisible join.

With RS facing and bottom edge up, join A with a sl st in bottom edge in first row of rainbow band, dc along lower edge of rainbow band, then join using invisible join at front edge. Sew in remaining ends.

Sew buttons to left front opposite button loops.

Rainbow Striped Sun Hat

Absolutely adorable, the Rainbow Striped Sun Hat features a simple double crochet brim to protect baby's face and neck from the summer sun. Add a set of ties to secure it in place and make your baby the cutest one in town.

YOU WILL NEED

DK weight
60% cotton/40% acrylic
(140 m /153 yd, 50 g/ 1.75 oz)

* 2 balls of white (A)
* Small amounts in the
following colours:
red (B), bright yellow (C),
green (D), cobalt (E), purple (F)

EQUIPMENT
* 4 mm (US G/6) crochet hook
* 3.5 mm (US E/4) crochet hook
* Stitch marker
* Tapestry needle

TENSION
16 sts and 12 rounds = 10 cm (4")
in half treble crochet

SIZE
Size: Newborn [3–6 months]
Head circumference:
35.5 [43] cm (14 [17]")

SPECIAL STITCHES
* Standing dc (see page 114)
* Standing htr (see page 115)

TO MAKE

Crown

Use a stitch marker to keep track of the beginning of rounds and move the marker up as you work.
With larger crochet hook and A, make a magic ring.
Round 1: 2ch (counts as htr), work 7htr into ring. (8 sts)
Round 2: 2htr in each st to end. (16 sts)
Round 3: *2htr in next st, 1htr in next st; repeat from * to end. (24 sts)
Round 4: *2htr in next st, 1htr in next 2 sts; repeat from * to end. (32 sts)

Round 5: *2htr in next st, 1htr in next 3 sts; repeat from * to end. (40 sts)
Round 6: *2htr in next st, 1htr in next 4 sts; repeat from * to end. (48 sts)
Round 7: *2htr in next st, 1htr in next 11 [5] sts; repeat from * to end. (52 [56] sts)

Size Newborn only

Rounds 8–13: 1htr into each st to end. Break off yarn A and join with an invisible join at end of last round.

Size 3–6 months only

Round 8: *2htr in next st, 1htr in next

When you work the invisible join for the Rainbow Band, do not eliminate the back bar of the htr stitch you are working over when you weave in the ends. You will need the back bar to work the next round of the rainbow. You can fudge this by working into the yarn you have 'woven in' if necessary, but it helps to know this could cause an issue. If you do not want to work the htr in the back bar for these rounds, you can work htr stitches in the regular loops. It will still give you the striped effect but the stitches will not be as distinct as in the hat sample.

6 sts; repeat from * to end. (64 sts)

Rounds 9–15: 1htr in each st around. Break off yarn A and join with an invisible join at end of last round.

Rainbow Band

Next round: With larger crochet hook, join B with standing htr in back bar of any st, htr in back bar of each st around. Break off yarn B and join with an invisible join. (52 [64] sts)

Next round: Join C and repeat last rnd.

Next round: Join D and repeat last rnd.

Next round: Join E and repeat last rnd.

Next round: Join F and repeat last rnd.

Next round: Join A with standing dc in back bar of any st, 1dc in back bar of each st around. Do not join. Work

should measure approximately 12.5 [16] cm (5 [6¼]") from centre of crown.

Brim

Change to smaller hook.

Round 1: *1dc in next st, 2dc in next st; repeat from * to end. (78 [96] sts)

Rounds 2 and 3: 1dc in each st to end.

Round 4: * 2dc in next st, 1dc in next 2 sts; repeat from * to end. (104 [128] sts)

Rounds 5 and 6: 1dc in each st to end.

Round 7: * 2dc in next st, 1dc in next 3 sts; repeat from * to end. (130 [160] sts)

Rounds 8 and 9: 1dc in each st to end.

Round 10: Sl st in each st to end. Break off yarn A and join with an invisible join.

Sew in ends.

FINISHING

Ties (make 2, optional)

With smaller crochet hook and WS facing, join A with standing dc in any st of stripe in E on inside of hat.

Row 1: 60ch, beg in second ch from hook and work 1 sl st in back bump of each ch working back towards the hat. Break off neatly to inside loops of hat.

Count 26 [32] sts first tie and work second tie in same way as first.

If your hat becomes misshapen, lightly block it flat (see page 121).

Citrus Nappy Cover

This bright and cheerful striped nappy cover mixes summery citrus colours
with bright white to really make the design pop!

YOU WILL NEED

DK weight
60% cotton/ 40% acrylic
(140 m/153 yd, 50 g/1.75 oz)

∗ 1 ball in the following colours:
bright yellow (A), white (B),
red (C), orange (D), grass green (E)

EQUIPMENT
∗ 4 mm (US G-6) crochet hook
∗ Tapestry needle
∗ 2 x velcro strips
6.5 cm (2½") long
∗ 2 x 13 mm (½") buttons
(optional)
∗ Sewing needle and matching
thread

TENSION
∗ 16 sts and 8 rows = 10 cm (4") in
treble crochet

SIZE
Size: 3 [6] months
Waist circumference:
45.5 [48.5] cm (18 [19]")
Shown in size 3 [6] months.

TO MAKE

Back

Foundation ch: Using C, work 43
[47]ch.
Row 1: Beg in fourth ch from hook
(counts as tr), 1tr into each ch to end,
turn. (41 [45] sts)
Row 2: 3ch (counts as tr), 1tr into
each st to end, turn. Break off yarn.
Row 3: Join yarn B and 2ch (counts as
htr), 1htr in each st to end, turn.
Rows 4 and 5: Repeat row 3.
Break off yarn.
Rows 6 and 7: Join yarn D and repeat
row 2. Break off yarn at end of last row.

Row 8: Join yarn B, 2ch, miss next st,
1htr into next st (counts as htr2tog),
1htr up to last 2 sts, htr2tog, turn.
(39 [43] sts)
Row 9: 2ch, miss next st, 1htr into
next st, 1htr up to last 2 sts, htr2tog,
turn. (37 [41] sts)
Row 10: 2ch, miss next st, 1htr into
next st, 1htr up to last 2sts, 2htrtog,
turn. Break off yarn. (35 [39] sts)
Row 11: Join yarn A, 3ch, miss next st,
1tr into next st (counts as 2trtog), 1tr
up to last 2sts, 2trtog, turn. (33 [37] sts)
Row 12: Work as row 11. Break off
yarn. (31 [35] sts)
Row 13: Join yarn B, work as row 10.
(29 [33] sts)
Rows 14 and 15: Repeat row 10.
Break off yarn. (25 [29] sts)
Rows 16 and 17: Join yarn E, 2ch,
miss next st, 1tr into next st, 1tr up to
last 2 sts, tr2tog, turn. Break off yarn.
(21 [25] sts)

Front

Row 18: Join B, 1ch, 1htr to end, turn.

Rows 19 and 20: Rep row 18. Break off yarn.

Row 21: Join A, 3ch, 1tr to end, turn.

Row 22: Repeat row 21. Break off yarn.

Rows 23–25: Repeat rows 18–20.

Rows 26 and 27: Repeat rows 21 and 22.

Rows 28–30: Repeat Rows 18–20.

Row 31: Join A, ch 3, 1tr in same st (counts as tr increase), 1tr upto last st, 2tr into last st, turn. (23 [27] sts)

Row 32: Repeat row 31. Break off yarn. (25 [29] sts)

Rows 33–35: Repeat rows 18–20. Break off yarn at end of last row.

Velcro Waistband

The waistband is worked into the sides of Rows 1–5.

Row 1: Holding work with red stripe at top, with yarn A and WS facing, join yarn with a sl st in bottom of white stripe, 1ch, work 10dc along top edge, turn. (10 sts)

Row 2: 1ch, 1htr to end, turn.

Repeat last row 11 [14] more times. Break off yarn.

Repeat along other side of back.

Button Closure Waistband

Work in same way as velcro waistband until 10 [13] rows have been worked.

Buttonhole row 1: 2ch, 3htr, 2ch,

miss next 2 sts, 1htr into next st, then into each st to end, turn.

Buttonhole row 2: 2ch, 3htr, 1htr into each ch, 1htr into next st, then into each st to end, turn.

Next row: 1ch, 1htr to end. Break off yarn. Repeat along other side of back.

FINISHING

Edging

With yarn A and WS facing, work 1 round of dc along all edges, working 3dc in each corner. Break off yarn.

Sew in all ends.

Sew hook portion of tape to front flap and loop portions of tape to each end of waistband.

Sew buttons to front flap under buttonholes.

Snuggly Monster Mitts

Add a little playfulness to these colourful mittens by creating a monster face! These mitts feature a drawstring tie closure to easily fit on your little one's hands.

YOU WILL NEED

DK weight
60% cotton/40% acrylic
(140 m/153 yd, 50 g/1.75 oz)

* 1 ball of white (A)
* Small amounts in the
  following colours:
  red (B), bright yellow (C),
  green (D), cobalt (E), purple (F)

EQUIPMENT

* 4 mm (US G/6) crochet hook
* 2.25 mm (US B/1) crochet hook
* Small amounts of embroidery
  floss in colours black, white, red,
  and purple
* Tapestry needle

TENSION

16 sts and 12 rounds = 10 cm (4")
in half treble crochet

SIZE

Size: Newborn [3–6 months]
Hand circumference:
12.75 [15] cm (5 [6]")
Length: 9 [9.5] cm (3½ [3¾]")
Shown in size Newborn.

TO MAKE

Mitts (make 2)

Round 1: With larger crochet hook and B, 3ch, work 7 [8] htr into third ch from hook, join with a sl st in first htr. (7 [8] sts)

Round 2: 2ch, 2htr in each st to end, join with a sl st in first htr. (14 [16] sts)

Round 3: 2ch, * 2htr in next st, 1htr in next st; repeat from * to end. Break off yarn and close round with invisible join. (21 [24] sts)

Round 4: Join A with standing htr, 1htr in each st to end.

SPECIAL STITCHES

* Standing dc (see page 114)
* Standing htr (see page 115)
* BLO (see page 114)

Round 5: 1htr in each st to end. Repeat round 5 three [four] more times. Work should measure approximately 7 [7.5] cm (2¾ [3]").

Cuff

Next round: Join B with standing hdc in back bar of any st, hdc in back bar each st around. Cut B and join with an invisible join. (21 [24] sts)

Next round: Join C and repeat last rnd.

Next round: Join D and repeat last rnd.

Next round: Join E and repeat last rnd.

Next round: Join F and repeat last rnd.

Next round: Join A and repeat last rnd.
Sew in ends.

FINISHING

Ties (make 2)

With larger crochet hook, work 50 [55] ch. Break off yarn and sew in.

Weave tie in and out between posts of last round of cuffs. Tie in a bow.

Eyes (make 4)

Foundation ring: With smaller crochet hook and black embroidery thread, make a magic ring.

Round 1: 2ch, work 7htr in ring. Break off thread and join with an invisible join. (8 sts)

Round 2: Join white embroidery thread with a standing sc, leaving a 10 cm (4") long tail, work 1 more dc in same st, then 2dc in each st to end. Do not join. (16 sts)

Round 3: Sl st in each st to end. Break off thread and join with an invisible join. Sew in all ends.

Horns (make 4)

Foundation ch: With smaller crochet hook and red embroidery thread, work 8ch, leaving a 10 cm (4") long tail.

Row 1: Beg in second ch from hook, 1dc in next 3ch, 1htr in next 4ch, turn. (7 sts)

Row 2: 2ch, 1htr in next 4htr, 1dc in next 3dc, turn.

Row 3: 1ch, 1sc in next 3dc, 1htr in next 4htr, turn.

Row 4: Fold in half to form a long

tube, work sl st through both layers of foundation ch and last row. Break off.

Make 1 more horn with red embroidery thread, then 2 with purple embroidery thread.

Using yarn tails from eyes and horns, sew pieces to mittens as shown in photo. Sew in remaining ends.

Spring Stripes Dress

This petite, beautiful dress is perfect for the spring! Make the matching leggings on page 34 to complete the outfit.

YOU WILL NEED

4 ply weight
100% cotton
(63 m/69 yd, 25 g/0.88oz)

* 3 [4] balls of lemon yellow (A)
* 1 ball in the following colours:
coral (B), pink (C), cyan (D)

EQUIPMENT

* 3.5mm (US E/4) crochet hook
* Tapestry needle

TENSION

16 sts and 8 rows = 10 cm (4")
in treble crochet

SIZE

Size: 3 [6] months
Chest: 40 [42] cm (15¾ [16½]")
Length: 30.5 [33] cm (12 [13]")

TO MAKE

Yoke

Foundation ch: With B, work 71 [76] ch, join with a sl st in first ch, taking care not to twist ch.

Round 1: 3ch (counts as tr), 1tr in next 7 [8] ch, work (1tr, 1ch, 1tr) in next ch, *tr in next 17 [18] ch, work 9 (1tr, 1ch, 1tr) into next ch; repeat from * 2 more times, 1tr to end, join with a sl st in 3ch at beg of round. Break off. (79 [84] sts)

Round 2: Join yarn C, work 3ch (counts as tr), * 1tr in ch sp, work (1tr, 1ch, 1tr) in next ch sp; repeat from * 3 more times, 1tr to end, join with a sl st in 3ch at beg of round. Break off. (87 [92] sts)

Round 3: Join D, * 1tr first ch sp,

work (1tr, 1ch, 1tr) into next ch sp; repeat from * 3 more times, 1tr to end, join with a sl st in 3ch at beg of round. Break off yarn. (95 [100] sts)

Round 4: Join A, 3ch (counts as tr), * 1tr in 1ch sp, work (1tr, 1ch, 1tr) in next 1ch sp; repeat from * 3 more times, tr to end, join with a sl st in 3ch at beg of round.

Rounds 5–7: Repeat round 4 three more times. Break off yarn at end of last round. (127 [132] sts; 30 [32] sts for back, 31 [32] sts for front, 31 [32] sts for each sleeve, and 4 ch sps)

Body

Round 8: With RS facing, fold yoke so first 1chsp and second 1chsp meet, join A with a sl st through both ch sps, 3ch (counts as tr), 1tr into 1st before next 1chsp, 3ch, sl st in next st, line up third 1chsp with fourth 1chsp, sl st through both ch sps, 3ch, tr to end, join with a sl st in 3ch at beg of round. (63 [66] sts)

Round 9: 3ch (counts as tr), 1tr in

each st to end, join with a sl st in into 3ch at beg of round. Repeat round 9 four [six] times.

Increase round: 3ch (counts as tr), 1tr in next 5 [4] sts, 2tr in next st, *tr in each of next 6 [5] sts, 2tr in next st; repeat from * to end, join with a sl st in 3ch at beg of round. (72 [77] sts)

Work 1 round of tr.

Increase round: 3ch (counts as tr), 1tr next 7 [5] sts, 2tr in next st, *1tr in next 8 [6] sts, 2tr in next st; repeat from * around, join with a sl st in 3ch at beg of round. (80 [88] sts) Work 1 round of tr.

Increase round: 3ch (counts as 1tr), 1tr in next 8 [6] sts, 2tr in next st, *1tr in next 9 [7] sts, 2tr in next st; repeat from * around, join with a sl st in 3ch at beg of round. (88 [99] sts)

Work straight until piece measures 21 [23.5] cm (8¼ [9¼]") from armhole. Break off yarn.

Next round: Join C, 1ch, 1fpdc around the post of first st, *1bpdc around the post of the next st, 1fpdc around the post of the next st; Rep from * around, join with a sl st in beg dc.

Last round: 1bpdc around the post of first st, *1fpdc around the post of the next st, 1bpdc around the post of the next st. Rep from * to end, join with a sl st in dc at beg of round. (88 [99] sts)

FINISHING

Sew in ends. Block to measurements.

Spring Stripes Leggings

This adorable pair of leggings will look great teamed with a cute pastel top or under the matching dress on page 32.

YOU WILL NEED

4 ply weight
100% cotton
(63 m/69 yd, 25 g /0.88 oz)

* 2 balls of lemon yellow (A)
* 1 ball in the following colours: pink (B), cyan (C), coral (D)

EQUIPMENT

* 3.5mm (US E/4) crochet hook
* Tapestry needle

TENSION

20 sts and 18½ rows = 10 cm (4")
in double crochet
16 sts and 8 rows = 10 cm (4") in
treble crochet

SIZE

Size: 3 [6] months
Waist: 45.5 [48.5] cm (18 [19]")
Length: 33 [35.5] cm (13 [14]")

TO MAKE

Waistband

Foundation ch: With B, 11ch.
Row 1: Beg in second ch from hook, 1dc into each ch to end, turn. (10 sts)
Row 2: 1ch, 1dc into first st, 1dc into back loop of next 8 sts, 1dc in last st, turn.
Row 3-84 [88]: Rep row 2.
Joining row: Holding work with last row and foundation ch even, work sl st through edge of foundation ch to end of row, being careful not to twist work.

Hips

Turn work with one long edge at top.
Round 1: 1ch, work 84 [88] dc evenly around, join with a sl st in first dc. Break off yarn. (84 [88] sts)
Round 2: Join A, 3ch (counts as tr), 10 [9] tr, 2tr into next st, *11 [10] tr, 2tr into next st; repeat from * 4 [6] more times, 1tr to end, join with a sl st in 3ch at beg of round. (90 [96] sts)
Round 3: 3ch (counts as 1tr), 1tr into each st to end, join with a sl st in in 3ch at beg of round.
Rounds 4–7: Rep round 3. Work should measure 8.5 cm (3¼") from waistband.

First Leg

Dividing round: 3ch (counts as tr), 1tr into each of next 44 [47] sts, join with a sl st in 3ch at beg of round, leaving remaining 45 [48] sts unworked. (45 [48] sts)

Next round: 3ch (counts as tr), 1tr into each st to end, join with a sl st into 3ch at beg of round.

Continue even until leg measures 15 [18] cm (6 [7]"), or approximately 4.5 cm (1¾") (short of desired length. Fasten off A at end of last round.

Next round: Join C, 3ch, 1tr into each st to end, join with a sl st into 3ch at beg of round. Break off yarn.

Next round: Join D, 3ch, 1tr into each st to end, join with a sl st into 3ch at beg of round. Break off yarn.

Next round: Join B, 3ch, 1tr into each st to end, join with a sl st into 3ch at beg of round.

Next round: 1ch, 1dc in each st to end, join in dc at beg of round with an invisible join. Break off yarn.

Second Leg

Join A to remaining sts with a sl st, leaving a 30.5 cm (12") long tail. Work second leg in same way as first.

FINISHING

Sew in ends. Using long tail from second leg, sew crotch closed. Block to measurements (see page 121).

Walk in the Park Hoodie

This soft and snuggly hoodie is the perfect weight for playing outside on a chilly autumn evening. Mainly worked in treble crochet, it's quick and easy to make!

YOU WILL NEED

Aran weight
100% acrylic
(155 m/170 yd, 100 g/3.5 oz)

* 2 balls of cornflower blue (A)
* 1 ball of raspberry (B)
* 1 ball of bright yellow (C)

EQUIPMENT

* 6 mm (US J/10) crochet hook
* 3 locking stitch markers
* Tapestry needle

TENSION

11 sts and 7 rows = 10 cm (4")
in treble crochet

SIZE

Size: 6 months [12 months, 18 months]
Chest circumference: 53.5 [55, 57] cm (21 [21¾, 22½,]")
Length (hem to neck): 27.5 [29, 30.5] cm (10¾ [11½, 12]")

TO MAKE

Body

Foundation ch: With A, loosely work 58 [60, 62] ch, join with a sl st in first ch to form a circle, being careful not to twist chain.

Round 1 (WS [RS, WS]): 3ch (counts as tr) turn, 1tr in back bar of each ch around, join with a sl st in top of 1ch at beg of round..

Round 2: 3ch (counts as tr), turn, 1tr in each st around, join with a sl st in top of 1ch at beg of round..

Repeat last round 10 [11, 11] more times, ending with a RS [RS, WS] round. Body should measure 17 [19, 19] cm (6¾ [7½, 7½]") from beg.

Yoke

Round 1(WS [WS, RS]): Turn, sl st in first 2 sts, 3ch (counts as tr), 1tr in next 26 [26, 28] sts, work 16 [16, 19] ch for armhole, miss next 2 [3, 2] sts, tr in next 27 [27, 29] sts; ch 16 [16, 19] for armhole, miss remaining 1 [2, 1] st(s), join with a sl st in top of 3ch at beg of round. (86 [86, 96] sts; 27 [27, 29] sts each for front and back, and 16 [16, 19] sts for each sleeve).

Round 2: Turn, sl st in first st, 2ch (does not count as a st), 1tr into next ch, *1tr in next 12 [12, 15] ch, tr2tog, mark last st worked, tr2tog, 1tr in next 23 [23, 25] sts, tr2tog**, mark last st worked, tr2tog; repeat from * to **, join with a sl st in top of first tr. (78 [78, 88] sts)

Round 3: Turn, sl st in first st, 2ch (does not count as a st), 1tr in next

st, *1tr in each st up to 2 sts before marker, tr2tog, move marker to last st worked, tr2tog; repeat from * 2 more times, 1tr in each st up to last 2 sts, tr2tog, join with a sl st into top of first tr. (8 sts decreased)

Repeat last round 4 [4, 5] more times, ending with a WS row. (38 [38, 40] sts; 15 sts each for front and back, and 4 [4, 5] sts for sleeves).

Fasten off and remove all markers.

Mark st 7 [7, 34] st of the last round.

All sizes

Hood

With B and RS facing, join yarn in marked st with a sl st. Remove stitch marker.

Row 1 (RS): 3ch (counts as tr), in each st around up to last st, miss last st. Do not join. (37 [37, 39] sts)

Row 2: 3ch (counts as tr), turn, 1tr in each st to end.

Repeat last row 11 [12, 12] times.

Shape hood

Decrease row 1: 3ch (counts as tr), turn, 1tr in next 15 [15, 16] sts, tr2tog, 1tr in next st, tr2tog, 1tr in each st to end. (35 [35, 37] sts)

Decrease row 2: 3ch (counts as tr), turn, 1tr in next 14[14, 15] sts, tr2tog, 1tr in next st, tr2tog, 1tr in each st to end. (33 [33, 35] sts)

All sizes

Break off, leaving a long tail for sewing. Sew top of hood together along last row.

Edging round (RS): With B and RS facing, join yarn with a sl st in missed st at centre front, work 47 [51, 51] dc evenly spaced around front of hood, join with a sl st in first dc. Break off yarn.

Sleeves (make 2)

Round 1: With WS [RS, WS] facing, join A with a sl st at centre of underarm, 3ch (counts as tr), work 21 [22, 24] tr evenly spaced around armhole, join with a sl st in top of 3ch at beg of round. (22 [23, 25] sts)

Round 2: 3ch (counts as tr), turn, 1tr in next st and each st upto last 2 sts, tr2tog, join with a sl st in top of 3ch at beg of round. (21 [22, 24] sts)

Round 3: 3ch (counts as tr), turn, 1tr in next st and in each st around, join with a sl st into top of 3ch at beg of round.

Round 4: Turn, sl st in first st, 2ch (does not count as a st), 1dc in next st and each st to end, join with a sl st in top of first tr. (20 [21, 24] sts)

Round 5: Repeat round 3.

Repeat rounds 2–5 one more time. (18 [19, 21] sts)

Repeat round(s) 2–3 [2–4, 2–5] once more, ending with a WS round. (17 [17, 19] sts)

Next round (RS): Repeat round 3. Break off yarn.

Pocket

Foundation ch: With C, work 21[21,23] ch.

Row 1 (WS): Beg in second ch from hook, 1dc into each ch to end. (20 [20, 22] sts)

Row 2 (RS): 1ch (does not count as a st), turn, 1dc in each st to end.

Repeat last row 0 [0, 1] time(s).

Shape Sides

Decrease row 1: Turn, sl st in first st, 1ch (does not count as a st), 1dc in each st up to last st, miss last st. (18 [18, 20] sts). Mark first and last st of this row.

Next row: 1ch, turn, 1dc in each st to end.

Decrease row 2: 1ch (does not count as a st), turn, dc2tog, 1dc up to last 2 sts, dc2tog. Repeat last 2 rows 4 [4, 5] more times. (16 [16, 18] sts).

Work 1 [1, 0] more row of dc.

Edgings

With RS facing and working along shaped edge only, 1ch, work 12 [12, 13] dc evenly spaced along shaped edge to marked st. Break off yarn.

With C and RS facing, join yarn with a sl st in marked row on other side of pocket, working along shaped edge only, 1ch, work 12 [12, 13] dc evenly spaced along shaped edge to top of pocket. Break off yarn.

FINISHING

Sew in ends. Block pieces to measurements (see page 121).

Pin pocket to centre front, placing bottom of pocket at top of row 2. Sew pocket to body along top, bottom, and side edges, leaving shaped edges open.

GIFTS & TOYS

Hot Air Balloon Bunting

Add a pop of colour to the wall with these fun hot air balloons. You can adjust the length of the bunting to suit your style.

YOU WILL NEED

4 ply weight
100% cotton
(63 m/69 yd, 25 g/0.88 oz)

1 ball in the following colours: red (A), gold (B), teal (C), violet (D), sky blue (E), lime green (F)

EQUIPMENT

* 3.25 mm (US D/3) crochet hook
* 4 mm (US G/6) crochet hook
* Grey felt, approximately 30.5 cm (12") by 35.5 cm (14")
* Tapestry needle
* Upholstery needle

TENSION

Each balloon should measure 7 cm (2¾") wide and 8 cm (3¼") high before backing

SIZE

Length: 8 cm (3¼")
Width: 7 cm (2¾") (widest point of balloon)
Length of felt pieces: 10 cm (4")

TO MAKE

Balloons

Make 2 each in each of the following colours: A, B, C, D, and F.

Foundation ch: With smaller crochet hook, work 9ch.

Row 1: Beg in second ch from hook, 1dc in each ch to end, turn. (8 sts)

Row 2: 1ch, 1dc in each st to end, turn.

Row 3: 1ch, 2dc in first st, 1dc up to last st, 2dc in last st, turn. (10 sts)

Rows 4–9: Repeat Rows 2 and 3 three more times. (16 sts)

Row 10: 1ch, 1dc in first 3 sts, 1htr in next 3 sts, 1tr in next 4 sts, 1hdc in next 3 sts, 1dc in last 3 sts, turn.

Row 11: 1ch, 2dc in first st, 1dc up to last st, 2dc in last st, turn. (18 sts)

Row 12: 1ch, 1dc in next 3 sts, 1htr in next 3 sts, 2tr in next st, 1tr in next 4 sts, 2tr in next st, 1htr in next 3 sts, 1dc in next 3 sts, turn. (20 sts)

Row 13: 1ch, 1dc in next 2 sts, 1htr up to last 2 sts, 1dc in next 2 sts, turn.

Row 14: 1ch, miss first st, 1dc in next 3 sts, 1htr in next 3 sts, 2tr in next 4 sts, 2tr in next st, 1htr in next 3 sts, 1dc in next 2 sts, miss next st, 1dc in last st, turn.

Row 15: Repeat Row 14.

Row 16: 1ch, miss first st, 1dc in next 3 sts, 1htr in next 3 sts, 2tr in next st, 1tr in next 4 sts, 2tr in next st, 1htr in next 3 sts, 1dc in next 2 sts, miss next st, sl st in last st. Break off yarn.

Sew in ends.

Felt Backing

Using one of the balloons to create a template, cut 10 pieces of felt to back the shapes. The felt balloon should be slightly larger than the crochet balloon (excess can be trimmed away later).

Using the upholstery needle and contrasting colour yarn, sew each crochet balloon onto a piece of felt with running sts. Trim any excess felt from around the balloons.

Joining the Balloons

With 2 strands of sky blue and a 4 mm (US G/6) crochet hook, work 80ch. Sl st in central stitch of last row of first balloon. *work 25ch, sl st in central stitch of last row of next balloon; rep from * until all the balloons are attached, work 80ch. Break off.

Sew in ends by folding them over onto the chain and making an overhand knot with both the chain and the ends so that the ends are incorporated in the knot. Trim the ends close to the knot.

Little Bear Rattle

This cute bear rattle is great for baby girls or boys. Not only does it entertain your baby, but it also helps to develop fine motor skills, touch, and hearing.

YOU WILL NEED

4 ply weight
100% cotton
(63 m/69 yd, 25 g/0.88 oz)

* 1 ball of tan (A)
* Small amounts in the following colours: turquoise (B), cyan (C), lemon yellow (D), orange (E), rose pink (F)
Small amount of black yarn

EQUIPMENT

* 3 mm (US C/2) crochet hook,
* Polyester stuffing
* 3.5 cm (1½") diameter toy rattle
* Tapestry needle

TENSION

26 sts and 24 rounds = 10 cm (4") in double crochet

SIZE

Head circumference: 24 cm (9½")
Handle circumference: 11 cm (4¼")
Length: 20 cm (8")

TO MAKE

Ears (make 2)

Foundation ring: With A, make a magic ring.

Round 1: 1ch, 6dc into ring. Do not join. (6 sts)

Round 2: 2dc in each st to end. Do not join. (12 sts)

Round 3: * 1dc, 2dc in next st; repeat from * to end. Do not join. (18 sts)

Rounds 4–6: 1dc in each st to end. Join with a sl st at end of last round. Break off, leaving a long tail to sew.

Head

Foundation ring: With A, make a magic ring.

Round 1: 1ch, 6dc into ring. Do not join. (6 sts)

Round 2: 2dc in each st to end. Do not join. (12 sts)

Round 3: *1dc, 2dc in next st; repeat from * to end. Do not join. (18 sts)

Round 4: *2dc, 2dc in next st; repeat from * to end. Do not join. (24 sts)

Round 5: *3dc, 2dc in next st; repeat from * to end. Do not join. (30 sts)

Round 6: *4dc, 2dc in next st; repeat from * to end. Do not join. (36 sts)

Round 7: *5dc, 2dc in next st; repeat from * to end. Do not join. (42 sts)

Round 8: *6dc, 2dc in next st; repeat from * to end. Do not join. (48 sts)

Round 9: *7dc, 2dc in next st; repeat from * to end. Do not join. (54 sts)

Round 10: *8dc, 2dc in next st; repeat from * to end. Do not join. (60 sts)

Rounds 11–17: 1dc in each st to end. Do not join.

Round 18: *8dc, dc2tog; repeat from * to end. Do not join. (54 sts)

Round 19: *7dc, dc2tog; repeat from * to end. Do not join. (48 sts)

Round 20: *6dc, dc2tog; repeat from * to end. Do not join. (42 sts)

Round 21: *5dc, dc2tog; repeat from * to end. Do not join. (36 sts)

Round 22: *4dc, dc2tog; repeat from * to end. Do not join. (30 sts)

Sew ears to head as shown in photo, bending them slightly.

Using tapestry needle, embroider eyes with black yarn, using straight sts.

Embroider nose with F, using satin st to form an inverted triangle. Add a few sts in straight st for mouth.

Stuff head and insert rattle.

Round 23: *3dc, dc2tog; repeat from * to end. Cut A and use B to join round with a sl st in first dc. (24 sts)

Do not cut yarn at end of each subsequent round. Drop it to the back of work, and pick up the next colour.

Round 24: With B, ch 1, dc in each st around, drop B and use C to join with a sl st in first dc.

Round 25: With C, work 1ch, 1dc into each st to end, drop yarn C and use yarn D to join with sl st into first dc.

Round 26: With D, work 1ch, 1dc into each st to end, drop yarn D and use

yarn E to join with sl st into first dc.

Round 27: With E, work 1ch, 1dc into each st to end, drop yarn E and use yarn F to join with sl st into first dc.

Round 28: With F, work 1ch, 1dc into each st to end, drop yarn F and use yarn B to join with sl st into first dc.

Rounds 29–45: Firmly stuffing handle with stuffing every few rounds as you work; repeat rounds 24–28 three more times, then repeat rounds 24 and 25 once more. Cut all colours except C on the last repeat of that colour.

Round 46: With C, * 2dc, tr2tog, rep from * to end, join with a sl st in first dc. (18 sts)

Round 47: *1dc, 2dctog; repeat from * to end, join with a sl st in first dc. (12 sts)

Round 48: *dc2tog; repeat from * to end, join with a sl st in first dc. (6 sts)

FINISHING

Break off yarn. Add additional stuffing to tip of handle. Thread tail through top of remaining sts, then pull tight to close hole. Sew in ends.

Friendly Soft Toys

Soft, cuddly, and with long arms and legs, any little one will love to play with these two adorable friends. They are also perfect to give as a set.

YOU WILL NEED

4 ply weight
78% cotton/22% acrylic
(130 m/142 yd, 50 g/1.75 oz)

Bunny toy: 2 balls of lilac (A)
* 1 ball of cream (B) and amethyst (F)
* Small amounts in the following colours: duck egg (C), pale pink (D), mint green (E)
Dog toy: 2 balls of mint green (E)
* 1 ball of cream (B)
* Small amounts in the following colours: lilac (A), duck egg (C), pale pink (D), amethyst (F)

EQUIPMENT
* 4 mm (US G/6) crochet hook
* Tapestry needle
* Polyester stuffing

TENSION
19 sts and 21 rows = 10 cm (4") in double crochet

SIZE
Body circumference:
38 cm (15")
Length: 46.5 cm (18¼")

SPECIAL STITCHES
* Loop stitch (LS) (see page 113)

TO MAKE

Back

Foundation ch: With A for Bunny, and E for Dog, work 37ch.
Row 1: Beg in second ch from hook, 1dc in each st to end, turn. (36 sts)
Rows 2–46: 1ch, 1dc in each st to end, turn. Break off yarn at end of last row.

Front

Work same as back, leaving a long tail for sewing pieces together.

Eyes

Place marker at centre of front, 16 rows from the top edge. Insert hook from front to back, 4 sts to left of marker. Holding F for Bunny, and C for Dog in back of work, yarn over hook and pull through a loop. Working sl st along front of pieces, work 8 sts up toward top edge, 5 sts to the left, working the first and last at an angle to a curve, then 8 sts down to same row as beginning. Break off and pull yarn to back.

Beg 4 sts to right of marker, work remaining eye to match.

Add eyelashes if desired, using tapestry needle and same colour as eyes to embroider 2 sts per lash, using photo as a guide. Break off yarn.

Muzzle (Dog only)

Foundation ch: With A, work 12ch.
Round 1: Beg in second ch from hook, work 1dc into 10ch, 3dc in next ch, turn piece with remaining edge of ch

facing up, work 1dc into next 10ch, 3dc in next ch. Do not join. (26 sts)

Round 2: (10dc, 2dc in next st, 1dc, 2dc in next st) twice. Do not join. (30 sts)

Round 3: (11dc, 2dc in next st, 2dc, 2dc in next st) twice. Do not join. (34 sts)

Round 4: 11dc, 2dc in next st, 3dc, 2dc in next st, 12dc, 2dc in next st, 4dc, 2dc in next st, join with a sl st in next st. Break off yarn, leaving a long tail for sewing. (38 sts)

Sew muzzle to front just below eyes.

Tongue (Dog only)

Foundation ring: With D, make a magic ring.

Row 1: 1ch, 3dc in ring, do not join, and turn.

Row 2: 1ch, 2dc in each st, turn.

Row 3: 1ch, * 1dc, 2dc in next st; repeat from *.

Break off yarn, sew just below muzzle.

Nose

Foundation ring: With C for Bunny, and F for Dog, make a magic ring.

Row 1: 1ch, 3dc into ring, do not join, and turn.

Row 2: 1ch, 3dc, turn.

Row 3: 1ch, 1dc, 2dc in next st, 1dc, turn.

Row 4: 1ch, 1dc, work (2dc in next st) twice, 1dc. Break off yarn, leaving a long tail for sewing.

Sew nose to front as shown in photo.

Belly (Bunny only)

Foundation ch: With B, work 13ch.

Round 1: Beg in second ch from hook, 11LS, 3LS in next st, turn piece with remaining edge of ch at top, work 10LS, 2LS 10LS, 2LS. Do not join. (26 sts)

Round 2: 2LS in next st, 10LS, 2LS in each of next 3 sts, 10LS, 2LS in each of next 2 sts. Do not join. (32 sts)

Round 3: 2LS in each of next 2 sts, 10LS, 2LS in each of next 5 sts, 13LS, 2LS in each of next 2 sts. Do not join. (41 sts)

Round 4: 2LS in each of next 2 sts, 16LS, 2LS in each of next 3 sts, 18LS, 2LS in each of next 2 sts, join with a sl st in next st. Break off yarn, leaving a long tail for sewing. (48 sts)

Sew belly to front.

Rosy Cheeks (make 2, Bunny only)

Foundation ring: With D, make a magic ring.

Round 1: 1ch, 6dc into ring, join with a sl st in 1ch at beg of round. Break off yarn. (6 sts)

Round 2: Join E with a sl st in first dc, 1ch, 2dc in each st around, join with a sl st in first dc. Break off yarn, leaving a long tail for sewing. (12 sts)

Sew cheeks to each side of nose.

Ears (make 2)

Foundation ring: With A for Bunny,

and B for Dog, make a magic ring.

Round 1: 1ch, 6dc into ring. Do not join. (6 sts)

Round 2: 2dc in each st. Do not join. (12 sts)

Round 3: *1dc, 2dc in next st; repeat from * around. Do not join. (18 sts)

Round 4: *2dc, 2dc in next st; repeat from * around. Do not join. (24 sts)

Rounds 5–23: 1dc into each st to end, do not join. At end of last round, join with a sl st in next st. Break off yarn.

Ear Appliqué (make 2, Bunny only)

Foundation ch: With D, work 12ch.

Round 1: Beg in second ch from hook, 10dc, 3dc in last ch, turn piece with remaining edge of ch at top, 10dc, 1dc in 1ch at beg of round. Do not join. (24 sts)

Round 2: Sl st to beg of round 1, 1ch, 10dc, 2dc in each of next 3 sts, 11dc, join with a sl st in next st. Break off, leaving a long tail for sewing. (27 sts)

Sew appliqués to ears as shown in photo.

Ear Appliqué (Dog only)

Make several dots using D and C.

Foundation ring: Make a magic ring.

Round 1: 1ch, 6dc into ring. (6 sts)

Round 2: 2dc in each st to end, join with a sl st in next st. Break off, leaving a tail for sewing. (12 sts)

Sew dots randomly placed on ears.

Arms (make 2)

Foundation ring: With B, make a magic ring.

Round 1: 1ch, 6dc into loop, join with a sl st in first dc. (6 sts)

Round 2: 1ch, 2dc in each st to end, join with a sl st in first dc. (12 sts)

Rounds 3–5: 1ch, 1dc in each st around, join with a sl st in first dc.

Rounds 6–18: Change to A for Bunny, and E for Dog. 1ch, 1dc in each st to end, join with a sl st to first dc. Break off yarn, leaving a long tail to sew.

Legs (make 2)

Foundation ring: With B, make a magic ring.

Round 1: 1ch, 6dc into loop, join with a sl st in first dc. (6 sts)

Round 2: 1ch, 2dc in each st to end, join with a sl st in first dc. (12 sts)

Round 3: 1ch, * 1dc, 2dc in next st; repeat from * to end, join with a sl st in first dc. (18 sts)

Rounds 4–6: 1ch, 1dc in each st to end, cut B. With C, join with a sl st in first dc.

Round 7: 1ch, 1dc in back loop of each st to end, join with a sl st in first dc.

Round 8: 1ch, 1dc in each st to end, join with a sl st in first dc.

Change to A for Bunny, and E for Dog. Do not cut C; carry it up along the back of work.

Rounds 9 and 10: Repeat rounds 7 and 8.

Change to D, do not cut yarn used, carry it up along the back of work.

Rounds 11 and 12: Repeat rounds 7 and 8.

Pick up C from back of work.

Rounds 13 and 14: Repeat rounds 7 and 8.

Rounds 15–26: Repeat rounds 9–14 two more times. Break off each yarn at end of last repeat of that colour, leaving a long tail of C to sew.

Tail (Dog only)

Foundation ring: With F, make a magic ring.

Round 1: 1ch, 6dc into ring, join with a sl st in first dc. (6 sts)

Round 2: 1ch, 2dc in each st to end, join with a sl st in first dc. (12 sts)

Round 3: 1ch, * 1dc, 2dc in next st; repeat from * to end, join with a sl st in first dc. (18 sts)

Rounds 4–12: 1ch, 1dc in each st to end, join with a sl st in first dc.

Change to E, and do not break off F, carrying it up along the back of work.

Rounds 13–16: Repeat round 4 four times.

Drop E and pick up F.

Rounds 17–20: Repeat round 4 four times. Break off F at end of last round.

Pick up E.

Rounds 21–26: Repeat round 4 six times. Break off yarn at end of last round, leaving a long tail to sew.

Tail (Bunny only)

Make a small pompom with F.

FINISHING

Sew front and back of body together along sides and top.

Take stuffing and stuff Bunny's ears firmly, and Dog's ears very lightly. Sew ears to top of head as shown in photo, with Bunny's ears upward, and Dog's ears pointing downward.

Stuff arms and sew to each side of body. Stuff body and sew bottom closed. Stuff legs and sew to bottom of body.

Sew tail to lower back.

MAKING A POM POM

1. Cut out two doughnut shaped rings of cardboard measuring 6 cm (2.5") in diameter and place them back-to-back.
2. Thread a 1 m (39") strand of yarn through the middle of the circles and then start wrapping it around the rings.
3. Continue until the cardboard is completely covered with several layers of yarn.
4. Place the a pair of scissors between the cardboard discs and snip the wrapped yarn all the way round.
5. Slide a piece of yarn between the discs and tie it together tight. Remove the cardboard discs.

Textured Stacking Blocks

The bright, textured surfaces make these blocks fun and intriguing toys for any baby. Mix and match the motifs on each block to create a unique game for your little one.

YOU WILL NEED

DK weight
60% cotton/40% acrylic
(140 m/153 yd, 50 g/1.75 oz)

* 1 ball in the following colours:
red (A), turquoise (B), orange (C)
lime (D), fuchsia (E), yellow (F),
dark grey (G)

EQUIPMENT
* 3.5 mm (US E/4) crochet hook
* Five 10 cm (4") cubes of dense
  upholstery foam
* Bread knife or electric carving
  knife

TENSION
Each side block measures slightly
over 10 cm (4")

SIZE

11 x 11 x 11 cm (4⅜ x 4⅜ x 4⅜")

SPECIAL STITCHES

* Spike stitch (see page 116)

TO MAKE

Striped Side (make 1 for each block)

Foundation ch: With first colour, work 17ch.

Row 1: Beg in second ch from hook, 1dc in each ch to end, turn. (16 sts)

Rows 2–4: 1ch, 1dc in each st to end. At end of last row, break off.

Row 5: Join next colour with dc in first dc, dc in each dc to end, turn.

Rows 6–8: 1ch, 1dc in each st to end, turn. At end of last row, break off yarn.

Rows 9–16: Repeat rows 5–8 once more, changing colours every 4 rows.

Edging

Row 1: With contrasting colour, join with dc in top right corner of square, work (2ch, 1dc) in same st, *work 12dc evenly across edge to corner, work (1dc, 2ch 1dc) in corner st; repeat from * 2 more times, work 12dc evenly along remaining edge, join with a sl st in first dc. Break off. (14 sts on each side, and 4 corner ch2sp)

Row 2: Join next colour with dc in any corner, 2ch, 1dc in same corner, *work 14dc to next corner, work (1dc, 2ch, 1dc) in ch2sp; repeat from * 2 more times, work 14dc along remaining edge, join with a sl st in first dc. Break off. (16 sts on each side, and 4 corner ch2sp)

Berry Stitch Solid Side (make 1 for each block)

Foundation ch: With colour of choice work 16ch.

Row 1: Beg in second ch from hook, dc in each ch to end, turn. (15 sts)

Row 2: 1ch, 1dc in first st, (work (1dtr in next st, 1dc in next st) across, turn.

Row 3: 1ch, 1dc in first st, work (miss dtr, 2dc in next st) to end, across, turn.

Rows 4, 6, 8, 10, and 12: Repeat row 2.

Row 5: 1ch, 2dc in first st, (miss dtr, 2dc in next st) up to last st, 1dc in last st, turn.

Row 7: Repeat row 3.

Row 9: Repeat row 5.

Row 11: Repeat row 3.

Row 13: Repeat row 5. Break off yarn.

Edging

Work edging in same way as for Striped Side.

Wavy Side (make 1 for each block)

Foundation ch: With colour of choice for MC, work 14ch.

Row 1: Beg in second ch from hook, dc in each ch to end, turn. Break off yarn. (13 sts)

Row 2: With CC1 of choice, join with a dc in first st, (miss next 2 sts, 7dtr in next 2 sts, 1dc in next st) 2 times, turn. Break off yarn.

Row 3: Join MC with spike stitch over first dc, (dc in next 7 sts, spike st over next st) 2 times, turn. Break off yarn.

Row 4: With CC2 of choice, join with a sl st in first st, 4ch (counts as dtr), 3 dtr in same st, miss next 3 sts, 1dc in next st, miss next 3 sts, 7dtr in next st, miss next 3 sts, spike st over next st, miss next 3 sts, 4 dtr in last st, turn. Break off yarn.

Row 5: Join MC with a dc in first st, sc in next 3 sts, spike st in next st, dc in next 7 sts, spike st over next st, dc in last 4 sts, turn. Break off yarn.

Rows 6–9: Repeat rows 2-5.

Rows 10 and 11: Repeat rows 2 and 3.

Edging

Work edging same as for Striped side.

Ripple side (make 1 for each block)

Foundation ch: With first colour, work 21ch.

Row 1 (WS): Beg in second ch from hook, dc in next ch, (3dc in next ch, 1dc in next 2ch, miss next 2ch, 1dc in next 2ch), twice, 3dc in next ch, 1dc in next ch, dc2tog, turn. (21 sts)

Row 2 (RS): 1ch, miss first st, (1dc in next 2 sts, 3dc in next st, 1dc in next 2 sts, miss next 2 sts) twice, 1dc in next 2 sts, 3dc in next st, 1dc in next st, dc2tog, turn. Break off yarn.

Row 3: Join second colour with dc2tog, 1dc in next st, (3dc in next st, 1dc in next 2 sts, miss next 2 sts, 1dc in next 2 sts) twice, 3dc in next st, 1dc in next st, dc2tog, turn.

Row 4: Repeat row 2.

Rows 5 and 6: With third colour; repeat rows 3 and 4.

Rows 7 and 8: With fourth colour; repeat rows 3 and 4.

Rows 9 and 10: With fifth colour; repeat rows 3 and 4.

Rows 11 and 12: With sixth colour; repeat rows 3 and 4. Do not turn at end of last row.

Edging

Round 1: With RS facing, join remaining colour with a dc in first st, (2ch, 1dc) in same st, (miss next st, 1dc in next 3 sts, miss next st, 1dc in next 2 sts) 2 times, miss next st, 1dc in next 2 sts, miss next 2 sts, work work (1tr, 2ch 1tr) in next st to turn corner, work 12dc evenly spaced along side, work (2dc, 2ch, 2dc) in corner, (1tr in next st, miss next st, 1tr in next st, miss next st, 1dc in next 2 sts, miss next st) twice, 1tr in next st, miss next st, 1tr in next st, miss next st, (work (2dc, 2ch, 2dc) in corner, work 12 sts evenly along side, join with a sl st in first st. Break off yarn. (14 sts on each side, with 4 corner ch2sp)

Round 2: With next colour, work same as round 2 of Striped Side edging.

Flower Circles Side (make 2 for each block)

Foundation ring: With first colour, work 5ch, join with a sl st in first ch to form a ring (or make a magic ring).

Round 1 (RS): 3ch (counts as

1tr),15tr into ring, join with a sl st in top of 3ch at beg of round. Break off yarn. (16 sts)

Round 2 (WS): Turn work. Join next colour with dc in any st, 1dtr in same st, (1dc, 1dtr) in each st to end, join with a sl st in first 1dc. Break off yarn. (16 berry sts)

Round 3 (RS): Turn work. Join next colour with 1dc in any dc, 1ch, miss next dtr, (1dc in next st, 1ch, miss next dtr) to end, join with a sl st in first 1dc. Break off yarn. (16dc, 16 ch1sp)

Round 4 (RS): Do not turn. Join next colour with a sl st in any ch1sp, ch1sp, 3ch (counts as tr), work (1tr, 2ch, 2tr) in same sp, * 2htr in next ch1sp, 2dc in next ch1sp, 2htr in next ch1sp, work (2tr, 2ch, 2tr) in next ch1; repeat from * 2 more times, 2htr in next ch1sp, 2dc in next ch1sp, 2htr in next ch1sp, join with a sl st in top of 3ch at beg of round. Break off. (10 sts on each side, and 4 corner ch2sp)

Round 5 (WS): Turn work. Join next colour with 1dc in any corner ch2sp, (work 92ch, 1dc) in same sp, (1dtr in next st, 1dc in next st) 5 times, work (1dc, 2ch, 1dc) in next corner ch2sp; repeat from * 2 more times, (1dtr in next st, 1dc in next st) 5 times, join with a sl st in first 1dc. Break off yarn. (12 sts on each side, and 4 corner ch2sp)

Round 6 (RS): Turn work. Join next colour with 1dc in any corner ch2sp, work (2ch, 1dc) in same sp, *miss first 1dc, (2dc in next dc) 6 times, work (1dc, 2ch, 1dc) in next corner ch2sp; repeat from * 2 more times, skip next dc, (2dc in next dc) 6 times, join with a sl st in first dc. Break off yarn. (14dc on each side, and 4 corner ch2sp)

Round 7 (RS): Do not turn. Join next colour with dc in any corner ch2sp, work (2ch, 1dc) in same sp, *dc in each dc to corner ch2sp, work (1dc, 2ch, 1dc) in ch2sp; rep from * 2 more times, 1dc in each dc to corner, join with a sl st in first 1dc. Break off. (16 sts on each side, and 4 corner ch2sp)

FINISHING

Sew in ends. Block each square to measurements (see page 121).

Using a bread knife or electric knife, cut foam into 10 cm (4") cubes (some irregularities in cutting are fine since they will be covered).

Holding 2 blocks together and with colour of choice, work sl st through both layers along one edge. Hold another block with a corner at seam, sl st through both layers along one edge. Continue joining blocks to form a cube, breaking off and rejoining yarn as needed, and making sure to place flower circle sides on opposite sides of cube, and leaving at least 3 adjacent edges open. Insert block of foam, then join remaining edges. Break off yarn. Sew in remaining ends.

Sunny Day Headband

This cute little headband has interchangeable motifs that can be swapped to match your little one's outfit. A perfect project for using up leftover scraps of yarn.

YOU WILL NEED

4 ply weight
100% cotton
(63 m/69 yd, 25 g/0.88 oz)

* 1 ball in the following colours:
cream (A), red (B),
lemon yellow (C), lime green (D),
royal blue (E)
* Small amounts in the following
colours:
Cloud: sky blue (F)
Sun: bright yellow (G)

EQUIPMENT

* 3 mm (US C/2) crochet hook
* Tapestry needle

TENSION

Not important for this pattern

SIZE

Size: 6 months
Head circumference: 43 cm (17")
Width: 4.5 cm (1¾")

SPECIAL STITCHES

* Standing dc (see page 114)

TO MAKE

Headband

Foundation ch: With A, loosely work 80ch.

Row 1 (RS): Beg in second ch from hook, 1dc in each ch to end. Break off yarn. (79 sts)

Row 2 (RS): Join yarn B with a standing dc in first st, *ch 1, skip 1 st, dc in next st; rep from * to end of row. Fasten off.

Row 3 (RS): Join A with a standing dc in first st, 1dc in ch1sp, * 1ch, miss next st, 1dc in ch1sp, rep from * to last 2 sts, 1dc in ch1sp and last st. Break off yarn.

Row 4 (RS): Join C with a standing dc in first st, 1ch, miss next st, 1dc in ch1sp, repeat from * to last 2 sts, 1ch, miss next st, 1dc in last st. Break off.

Row 5 (RS): With A, repeat row 3.

Row 6 (RS): With D, repeat row 4.

Row 7 (RS): With A, repeat row 3.

Row 8 (RS): With E, repeat row 4.

Row 9 (RS): With A, repeat row 3, but do not cut yarn, 1ch, turn.

Row 10 (WS): * 1dc in next st, 1dc in ch1sp; repeat from * to end. Do not cut yarn.

FINISHING

Sew in ends. Hold headband with right sides together and short ends even. With yarn from last row, and working through both layers, *dc in A at row ends, 1ch, miss next row end; rep from * to last row, dc in last row end. Break off yarn.

Motifs

Cloud

Foundation ch: With F, work 10ch, leaving a long tail.

Row 1: Beg in third ch from hook, tr in each ch to end, 1ch, turn. (9 sts)

Row 2: Dc in each st to end, 1ch, turn.

Row 3: Work (1dc, 1htr, 1tr) in next st, 2tr in next st, work (1htr, 1dc) in next st, sl st in next st, work (1htr, 1tr) in next st, 3tr in next st, dc in next st, sl st in next 2 sts, rotate piece with side edge at top, work (1dc, 1htr, 1tr) in side of dc, tr over post of tr, turn work with foundation ch at top, work (1tr, 1htr) in next loop, dc in next 6 loops, dc in each ch of foundation ch, join with a sl st in next st. Break off yarn, leaving a long tail.

Use tapestry needle to weave ends to middle of cloud on WS. Use long tails to sew or tie motif to headband.

Sun

Foundation: With G, make a magic ring, leaving a long tail.

Round 1: 3ch (counts as tr), 15tr into ring, join with a sl st in top of 3ch at beg of round. (16 sts)

Round 2: 1dc in same sp as sl st, *8ch, sl st into third ch from hook, 5ch, 1dc in next st; repeat from * 14 more times, 8ch, sl st into third ch from hook, 5ch, join with a sl st in first st. Cut yarn, leaving a long tail. (16 loops for sun rays)

Use tapestry needle to sew ends to middle of sun on WS. Use long tails to sew or tie motif to headband.

ASSEMBLY

Select the motif of your choice and position on the front left-hand side. Use any leftover yarn from crocheting the motif and sew the motif tightly in place.

Pastel Chevron Hat

Soft and gentle rainbows are created with an easy chevron stitch pattern. The Pastel Chevron Hat is worked flat and cinched closed at the top.

YOU WILL NEED

DK weight
60% cotton/40% acrylic
(140 m/153 yd, 50 g/1.75 oz)

* 1 ball of white (A)
* Small amounts in the
  following colours:
  rose pink (B), lilac (C),
  baby blue (D), mint green (E),
  lemon yellow (F)

EQUIPMENT

* 4 mm (US G/6) crochet hook
* Tapestry needle

TENSION

16 sts and 8 rows = 10 cm (4") in
chevron pattern

SIZE

Size: Newborn [0–3 months, 6–12
months]
Brim circumference:
33 [38, 43] cm (13 [15, 17]")
Length: 14 [15, 16.5] cm
(5½ [6, 6½]"), with brim folded

SPECIAL STITCHES

* Standing tr (see page 115)

TO MAKE

Brim

Foundation ch: With A, work 10ch.
Row 1: Beg in second ch from hook,
work 1dc in back bump of each ch
across, 1ch, turn. (9 sts)
Row 2: 1ch (does not count as dc),
1dc in first st, 1dc in back loop only of
next 8 sts, 1dc in last st, 1ch, turn.

Repeat row 2 until work measures
33 [38, 43] cm (13 [15, 17]").

Hat

Row 1 (RS): Rotate brim with one
long edge up, and yarn at right end
of work. Work 48 [56, 64] dc evenly
across. Break off yarn, leaving an
20.5 cm (8") long tail for sewing.
Do not turn.

When adding each new colour yarn
for the chevron section, be sure to
leave a 15 cm (6") tail of yarn to seam
the hat.
Row 2 (RS): Join B with standing tr
in first st, work 1tr in base of same st,
1tr in next st, work (tr2tog) twice, tr in
next st. *2tr in each of next 2 sts, tr in
next st, work (tr2tog) twice, tr in next
st; repeat from * to last st. 2tr in last st,
changing to C on last yoh, turn.
(48 [56, 64] sts)
Row 3: With C, work 3ch (counts
as tr), work 1tr in base of same st as
3ch just worked. 1tr in next st, work
(tr2tog) twice, 1tr in next st, *2tr in
each of next 2 sts, 1tr in next st, work
(tr2tog) twice, 1tr in next st; repeat

Size 6–12 months only

Row 6: With F, repeat row 3, changing to B on last yoh, turn.

Row 7: With B, repeat row 3, changing to C on last yoh. turn.

Row 8: With C, repeat row 3, changing to A on last yoh, turn.

Sizes 0–3 [6–12] months only

Shape top.

Decrease row I: 3ch (counts as tr), tr2tog, * 1tr in next st, tr2tog; repeat from * to end, turn. (42 [48] sts)

Decrease row 2: 3ch (counts as tr), tr2tog, * 1tr in next st, tr2tog; repeat from * to end, turn. (28 [32] sts)

Decrease row 3: 3ch (counts as tr), *tr2tog; repeat from * to last st, dc in last st, turn. (15 [17] sts)

Decrease row 4: 3ch (counts as tr), *tr2tog; repeat from * to end. (8 [9] sts) Break off yarn, leaving a long tail for sewing.

All sizes

FINISHING

Thread tail through remaining sts and pull tight to close top. Beginning at crown of hat and working to brim, seam the side edges of the hat closed; change colours for each section as you work. Sew in remaining ends.

To wear, fold half of brim up to RS.

---

from * to last st. 2tr in last st, changing to D on last yoh, turn.

Row 4: With D, repeat row 3, changing to E on last yoh, turn.

Row 5: With E, repeat row 3, changing to F on last yoh, turn.

Size Newborn only

Row 6: With F, repeat row 3, changing to A on last yoh, turn.

Row 7: With A, repeat row 3.
Shape top.

Decrease row I: 3ch (counts as tr), tr2tog, * 1tr in next st, tr2tog; repeat from * to end, turn. (32 sts)

Decrease row 2: 3ch (counts as tr), * tr2tog; repeat from * to last st, 1tr in last st, turn. (17 sts)

Decrease row 3: 3ch (counts as tr), * tr2tog; repeat from * to end. (9 sts) Break off yarn, leaving a long tail for sewing.

Size 0–3 months only

Row 6: With F, repeat row 3, changing to B on last yoh, turn.

Row 7: With B, repeat row 3, changing to A on last yoh, turn.

Pastel Chevron Mittens

Flexible and lightweight, the simple drawstring closure allows you to gently secure the mittens to your baby's hands and protect them from their little nails.

YOU WILL NEED

DK weight
60% cotton/40% acrylic
(140 m/153 yd, 50 g/1.75 oz)

* 1 ball of white (A)
* Small amounts in the
  following colours:
  rose pink (B), lilac (C),
  baby blue (D), mint green (E),
  lemon yellow (F)

EQUIPMENT

* 4 mm (US G/6) crochet hook
* Tapestry needle

TENSION

16 sts and 8 rows = 10 cm (4") in
chevron pattern

SIZE

Size: Newborn [3–6 months]
Hand circumference:
12.5 [15] cm (5 [6]")
Length: 11.5 [12.5] cm (4½ [5]")

TO MAKE

Cuff

Foundation ch: With A, work 6ch.
Row 1: Beg in second ch from hook work dc in back bump of each ch across, 1ch, turn. (5 sts)
Row 2: Sl st in first st, sl st in back loop only of next 3 sts, sl st in last st, 1ch, turn.
Row 3: 1ch (does not count as dc), 1dc in first st, 1dc in back loop only of next 3 sts, 1dc in last st, 1ch, turn.
  Repeat rows 2 and 3 until piece measures 10 [12.5] cm (4 [5]").

SPECIAL STITCHES

* Standing tr (see page 115)
* Standing dc (see page 114)

Mitt

Row 1 (RS): Turn cuff with one long edge up, and yarn at right end of work. Work 20 [24] dc evenly across. Fasten off, leaving an 20.5 cm (8") long tail for sewing. Do not turn.
Row 2 (RS): Join B with standing tr in first st, work 0 [1] tr in base of same st, tr in next st, 2 [0] tr in next 1 [0] st, 1 [0] tr in next 1 [0] st, work (tr2tog) twice, tr in next st, *2tr in each of next 2 sts, tr in next st, work (tr2tog) twice, tr in next st; repeat from * 0 [1] more time, 2tr in next st, 1 [0] tr in next 2 [0] sts, changing to D [C] on last yoh, turn. (20 [24] sts)

Row 3: With D [C], 3ch (counts as tr), work 0 [1] tr in base of same st as 3ch at beg of row, tr in next st, 2 [0] tr in next 1 [0] st, 1 [0] tr in next 1 [0] st, work (tr2tog) twice, tr in next st, *2tr in next 2 sts, tr in next st, work (tr2tog) twice, tr in next st; repeat from * 0 [1] more time, 2tr in next st, 1 [0] tr in next 2 [0] sts, changing to E [D] on last yoh, turn.

Row 4: With E [D], repeat row 3, changing to F [E] on last yoh, turn.

Row 5: With F [E], repeat row 3. End size Newborn here, and change to F on last yoh for size 3–6 months only, turn.

Size Newborn only

Dec row 1 (RS): Join A with standing dc in first st, dc in next st, dc2tog, *dc in next 2 sts, dc2tog; repeat from * to end, 1ch turn. (15 st]

Dec row 2 (WS): 1ch (counts as dc), dc2tog, *dc in next st, dc2tog; repeat from * to end. Break off yarn, leaving a long tail for sewing. (10 sts)

Size 3–6 months only

Row 6: With F, repeat row 3 and break off yarn at end of row. Shape top.

Dec row 1 (RS): Join A with standing dc, dc2tog, *dc in next st, dc2tog; repeat from * to end, 1ch, turn. (16 sts remain)

Dec row 2 (WS): 1ch (counts as dc), dc2tog, *1dc in next st, dc2tog; repeat

from * to last st, 1dc in last st. Break off yarn, leaving a long tail for sewing. (11 sts)

All sizes

Make second mitt in same way as first.

FINISHING

Thread tail through remaining sts and pull tight to close top. Beginning at tip of mittens and working to cuff, seam the side edges of the mittens closed; change colours for each section as you work. Sew in ends.

Wrist Ties (make 2)

With F, work 60ch. Break off yarn and sew in ends.

Secure the centre of tie at centre back of mitt. Weave ends of tie through sts above cuff. Tie in a bow on front of mitt.

Gradient Floor Blanket

The swirl of colours that radiates from the blanket's centre will provide a focal point to your baby's nursery! The blanket can be easily modified into any size and shape.

YOU WILL NEED

Aran weight
100% wool
(200 m/220 yd, 100 g/3.5 oz)

* 4 balls of white (A)
* I ball in the following colours:
red (B), orange (C),
bright yellow (D),
lemon yellow (E), lime green (F),
apple green (G), cobalt (H),
cornflower blue (I), fuchsia (J),
baby pink (K), claret (L),
cyan (M), heather (N)

EQUIPMENT
* 4.5mm (US 7) crochet hook

TENSION
Each motif measures 7 cm (2¾")
in diameter, without edging

SIZE
110 x 110 cm (43 x 43")

SPECIAL STITCHES
* 4 tr popcorn stitch (see page 64)
* 5 tr popcorn stitch (see page 64)

TO MAKE

Motif

Start with a magic ring.
Round 1: 3ch, 4trPC, 2ch, * 5trPC, 2ch; repeat from * 4 more times, join with a sl st to top of 3ch at beg of round. [6 popcorns, 6 ch2sp]
Round 2: Sl st to next ch2sp, work (3ch, 4trPC, ch1, 5trPC, 3ch) in same ch2sp, * work (5trPC, 1ch, 5trPC, 3ch) in next ch2sp; repeat from * 4 more times, join with a sl st to top of beg-ch. Break off yarn. [12 popcorns, 6 ch3sp]
   Make 163 motifs, 13 each of colours B, C, D, E, F, G, H, I, and M; 12 motifs each of colours L and N; and 11 motifs each of colours J and K.

Joining

Beginning with the first motif at the upper left, work your way down in columns. When a column is complete, work the next column on the right, beginning again at the top and work your way down. Place colours in 13 columns, alternating 13 rows of 12 motifs each and 12 rows of 13 motifs each , and a final row of 7 motifs as shown in the diagram on page 65.

First Motif

Join A in a ch3sp, work (2htr, 2ch, 2htr) in ch3sp, * 1htr in 5trPC, 1htr in ch1sp, 1htr in 5trPC, work (3htr, 2ch, 2htr) in ch3sp; repeat from * 4 more times, 1htr in 5trPC, 1htr in 1chsp,

1htr in 5trPC, 1htr in 3chsp, join with a sl st in first htr. Break off yarn.

Subsequent Motifs

The motifs are joined in the ch2sp at each corner. Join A in a ch3sp, work (2htr, 1ch, sl st in ch2sp of motif to be joined into, 1ch, 2htr) in ch3sp, work to end of round as for first motif, joining additional corners as needed. Break off yarn.

FINISHING

Sew in ends. Block to measurements, pinning out corners of outer motifs.

POPCORN STITCH

2ch, in the next stitch make 4tr. Pull up a loop and take hook out of your work. Insert hook from front to back into the second beg ch, straight into the loop you just pulled up. Tighten yarn to your hook, yarn over, and pull through loop and beg ch. This tightens the 4tr at the top and makes it pop at the front. Of course you can make even larger popcorns by adding 1 or 2tr. By going in with your hook from back to front, you'll create a popcorn that pops at the back of your work.

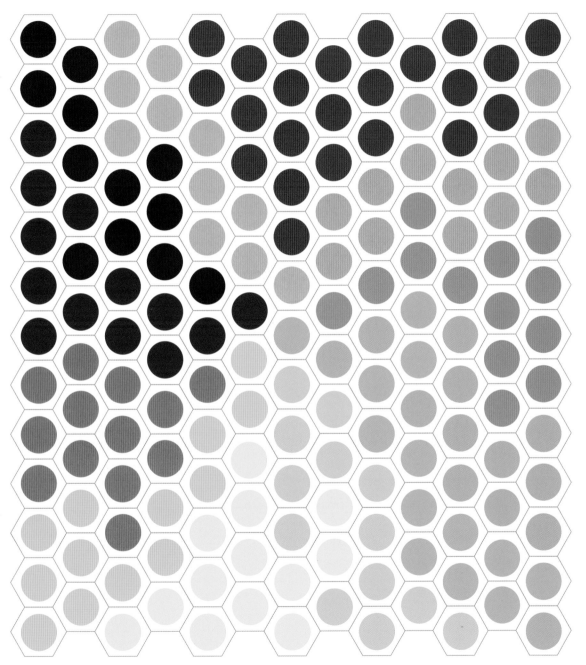

Key

- Claret (L), *12 motifs*
- Red (B), *13 motifs*
- Orange (C), *13 motifs*
- Bright yellow (D), *13 motifs*
- Lemon yellow (E), *13 motifs*
- Lime green (F), *13 motifs*
- Apple green (G), *13 motifs*
- Cyan (M), *13 motifs*
- Cobalt (H), *13 motifs*
- Cornflower blue (I), *13 motifs*
- Heather (N), *12 motifs*
- Fuchsia (J), *11 motifs*
- Baby pink (K), *11 motifs*

Pretty Mary Janes

The soft pastel colours used in this design make these shoes the perfect springtime gift. The little bows and buttons create adorable accents to this classic design.

YOU WILL NEED

Aran weight
100% cotton
(75 m/82 yd, 50 g/1.75 oz)

* 1 ball in the following colours:
ecru (A), lilac (B)
* Small amounts in the
following colours:
sky blue (C), lime green (D),
pale yellow (E), apricot (F)

EQUIPMENT

* 4 mm (US G/6) crochet hook
* Tapestry needle
* Two 15 mm (⅝") buttons

TENSION

17 sts and 13 rows = 10 cm (4") in
half treble crochet

SIZE

Size: 0–6 months
Foot circumference: 10 cm (4")
Foot length from heel:
8 cm (3¼")

TO MAKE

Sole

Foundation ch: With A, work 9ch.
Round 1: Work 3tr in third ch from hook, 1tr in each of next 5ch, 7tr in last chain, turn piece with remaining edge of foundation ch at top, 1tr in each of next 5ch, 3tr in last ch, join with a sl st in first tr. (23 sts)
Round 2: 2ch, 2tr in next 3 sts, 1tr in next 5 sts. 2tr in each of next 7 sts, 1tr in next 5 sts, 1tr in each of next 3 sts, join with a sl st in top of first tr. (36 sts)
 Break off yarn.

Upper

Round 1: With B and RS facing, 1ch, work 1htr in back loop only of each st to end, join with a sl st in first htr. (36 sts)
Round 2: 1ch, 1dc in each st to end, join with a sl st in first dc.
Round 3: 1ch, 1dc in next 10 sts, htr2tog 3 times, htr in next 4 sts, htr2tog 3 times, 1dc to end, join with a sl st in first 1dc. (30 sts remain)
Round 4: 1ch, 1dc in next 6 sts, 1htr in next st, tr2tog 6 times, 1htr into next st, 1dc to end, join with a sl st in first 1dc. (24 sts remain)
 Break off yarn. Sew in all ends.

Straps (make 2)

Foundation ch: With B, work 16ch.
Row 1: Beg in sixth ch from hook work 1htr in next st to form button loop, then 1htr to end. Break off yarn, leaving a long tail for sewing.

Bow

Foundation ch: With B, work 10ch.

Row 1: Beg in second ch from hook, 1htr in each ch to end, change to C.

Row 2: 2ch, turn, 1htr in each st to end, change to D.

Row 3: 2ch, turn, 1htr to end, change to E.

Row 4: 2ch, turn, 1htr to end, change to F.

Row 5: 1ch, turn, 1htr to end, change to B.

Row 6: 1ch, turn, 1htr to end. Break off.

FINISHING

Sew in all ends.

Sew one strap to each shoe, making sure straps are on opposite sides to each other. Sew a button to each shoe on opposite straps.

Pinch centre of bow together using photo as a guide, sew a few sts around centre of bow with B, then sew bow to shoe.

BOBBLE STITCH

With MC, insert hook in next st, yoh and pull through a loop (2 loops on hook), drop MC and pick up CC, yoh and pull through both loops on hook, working into same st just worked into (yoh, insert hook in st and pull up a loop, yo and pull through 2 loops on hook) 5 times (6 loops on hook), drop CC and pick up MC, yoh and pull through all loops on hook. (1 st remains on hook)

Bobble Pacifier Cords

Fun and function combined! These pacifier cords come together very quickly. So why limit yourself to only one when you can have a cord in every colour?

YOU WILL NEED

Aran weight
100% wool
(200 m/200 yd, 100 g/ 3.5 oz)

* 1 ball of white (MC)
* Small amount in the colour of your choice (CC)

EQUIPMENT

* 4.5 mm (US 7) crochet hook
* Tapestry needle
* Fastener clip

TENSION

16 sts = 10 cm (4") in double crochet

SIZE

Width: 3 x 22 cm (1¼ x 8¾")

SPECIAL STITCH

* Bobble stitch (see page 68)

TO MAKE

Cord

Foundation ch: With MC, work 36ch.
Row 1: Beg in second ch from hook, 1dc in each ch to end, 1ch, turn. (35 sts)
Row 2: 1dc in each st to end, 1ch, turn.
Row 3: 2dc, *make bobble, 2dc; repeat from * 10 more times, 1ch, turn. Break off CC.
Row 4: Repeat row 2.
Row 5: 1dc in each st to end, 1ch, rotate piece with end of rows at top edge, 1dc in end of each row, 1ch, turn.
Row 6: Along end, work dc2tog, 1dc, dc2tog. Cut yarn, leaving a long tail.

Loop

With MC, work 25ch. Break off yarn, leaving long tails at each end of ch.

FINISHING

Sew clip to shaped end of cord using long tail. Sew both ends of loop at other end of cord at row 3.

HANDY HINT

When working row 3, hold the contrasting colour along the top of row 2 and work the double crochet with A over the top of the contrast colour.

FOR THE NURSERY

Whatever the Weather Wall Hanging

This fun, colourful wall hanging will liven up any nursery! The bright, twirling 3-D shapes will be sure to excite and fascinate your little one.

YOU WILL NEED

Aran weight
100% acrylic
(389 m/425 yd, 197 g/7 oz)

* Small amounts in the following colours:
white (A), yellow (B), orange (C), blue (D), green (E), red (F), light blue (G), gold (H)

EQUIPMENT
* 4 mm (US G/6) crochet hook
* Polyester stuffing
* Stitch markers
* Tapestry needle
* Sewing needle
* Wooden mobile frame
* Super glue (optional)

TENSION
Varies between motifs

SIZE
Cloud: 7.75 x 6.5 cm
(3 x 2½")
Sun: 13 x 13 cm (5 x 5")
Rainbow: 17.5 x 7.75 cm
(6½ x 3")
Raindrop: 2.25 x 4 cm (1 x 1½")
Star: 13 x 10 cm (5 x 4")

SPECIAL STITCH
* Picot: work 3ch, sl st in first ch

TO MAKE

Cloud (make 2)
Round 1: 1ch in ring, work 8dc in ring, do not join. Pull tail to close centre. (8 sts)
Round 2: 2dc in each st to end, do not join. (16 sts)
Round 3: *1dc in next st, 2dc in next st; repeat from * to end, do not join. (24 sts)

Round 4: *1dc in next 2 sts, work (2htr in next st, 1htr in next st) twice, 2dc in next st, 1dc in next 2 sts, 2dc in next st; repeat from * once more, do not join. (32 sts)
Round 5: 1dc in next 3 sts, 2dc in next st, 1htr in next 3 sts, 2htr in next st, 1htr in next 2 sts, 1dc in next st, work (2dc in next st, 1dc in next 3 sts) twice, 2htr in next st, 1htr in next 3 sts, 2htr in next st, 1dc in next 3 sts, 2dc in next st, 1dc in next 3 sts, 2dc in next st, do not join. (40 sts)
Rounds 6 and 7: 1dc in each st to end, do not join.
Round 8: 1dc in next 3 sts, dc2tog, 1htr in next 3 sts, htr2tog, 1htr in next 2 sts, 1dc in next st, dc2tog, 1dc in next 3 sts, dc2tog, 1dc in next 3 sts, htr2tog, 1htr in next 3 sts, htr2tog, work (1dc in next 3 sts, dc2tog) twice do not join. (32 sts)
Round 9: *1dc in next 2 sts, htr2tog, 1htr in next 2 sts, htr2tog, 1htr in next 2 sts, dc2tog, 1dc in next 2 sts, dc2tog;

repeat from * once more, do not join. (24 sts)

Round 10: *1dc in next st, dc2tog; repeat from * to end, do not join. (16 sts)

Round 11: [dc2tog] around, do not join. (8 sts)

Stuff cloud, shaping the bumps in the cloud. Break off yarn and weave tail through the top of remaining sts, then pull tight to close hole. Sew in ends.

Sun (make 1)

Body

With B, make a magic ring.

Round 1: 1ch in ring, work 8dc in ring, do not join. Pull tail to close centre. (8 sts)

Round 2: 2dc in each st to end, do not join. (16 sts)

Round 3: *1dc in next st, 2dc in next st; repeat from * to end, do not join. (24 sts)

Round 4: *1dc in next 2 sts, 2dc in next st; repeat from * to end, do not join. (32 sts)

Round 5: *1dc in next 3 sts, 2dc in next st; repeat from * to end, do not join. (40 sts)

Rounds 6–11: 1dc in each st to end, do not join.

Round 12: *1dc in next 3 sts, dc2tog; repeat from * to end, do not join. (32 sts)

Round 13: *1dc in next 2 sts, dc2tog; repeat from * to end, do not join. (24 sts)

Round 14: *1dc in next st, dc2tog; repeat from * to end, do not join. (16 sts)

Stuff sun tightly.

Round 15: Work (dc2tog) to end, do not join. (8 sts)

Break off yarn and weave the tail through the top of remaining sts, then pull tight to close hole. Sew in ends.

Sun Rays

Row 1 (RS): Beg in second ch from hook, * work (sl st, 1dc) in next st, 1picot, work (1dc, sl st) into next st, sl st in next st, work (1dc, 1htr) in next st, work (1tr, 1dtr) in next st, 1picot, work (1dtr, 1tr) in next st, work (1htr, 1dc) in next st, 1dc in next st; repeat from * 4 more times, ** work (1dc, 1htr) in next st, work (1tr, 1dtr) in next st, 1picot, work (1dtr, 1tr) in next st, work (sl st, 1dc) in next st, 1picot, work (1dc, sl st) in next st, sl st in next st; repeat from ** 4 more times. (10 large rays and 10 small rays)

Break off yarn, leaving a long tail for sewing. Fold ray in half with WS tog. Using the long tail, sew top edges tog, making sure rays match, sew the bottom tog along foundation ch. Sew rays to sun, centring along the widest part, and with ends meeting. Sew in ends.

Rainbow (make 2)

Foundation ch: With D, work 32ch leaving a long tail, join with a sl st in first ch, being careful not to twist.

Round 1: 1ch, *1htr in next 3 sts, 2 htr in next st; repeat from * to end. With E, join with a sl st in top of first htr. Break off D. (40 sts)

Round 2: 1ch, *1htr in next 4 sts, 2 htr in next st; repeat from * to end. With B, join with a sl st in top of first htr. Break off E. (48 sts)

Round 3: 1ch, *htr in next 5 sts, 2 htr in next st; repeat from * to end. With C, join with a sl st in top of first htr. Break off B. (56 sts)

Round 4: 1ch, *1htr in next 6 sts, 2 htr in next st; repeat from * to end. With F, join with a sl st in top of first htr. Break off C. (64 sts)

Round 5: 1ch, *1htr in next 7 sts, 2 htr in next st; repeat from * to end, join with a sl st in top of first htr. Do not break off yarn. (72 sts)

Sew in ends, except for long tail of foundation ch. Fold ring in half to form an arch.

Using long tail from foundation ch, sew inner curve of arch closed.

With F, dc together edges of outer curve, working through both sts. When about three-quarters of the edge has been joined, begin stuffing rainbow. Continue working dc to end and stuff as you go. Break off yarn. Sew in ends.

Rain Drops (make 3)

Round 1: 1ch in ring, work 8dc in ring, do not join. Pull tail tight to close centre. (8 sts)

Round 2: 2dc in each st to end, do not join. (16 sts)

Rounds 3 and 4: 1dc in each st around, do not join.

Round 5: *1dc in next 2 sts, dc2tog; repeat from * to end, do not join. (12 sts)

Round 6: *1dc in next st, dc2tog; repeat from * to end, do not join. (8 sts)

Stuff rain drop.

Round 7: Work (dc2tog) to end, do not join. (4 sts)

Break off yarn and sew the tail through the top of remaining sts, then pull tight to close hole. Sew in ends.

Star (make 2)

Front

With H, make a magic ring.

Round 1: 1ch in ring, work 5dc in ring, join with a sl st in top of first dc. (5 sts)

Round 2: 1ch, 2dc in each st to end, join with a sl st in top of first dc. (10 sts)

Round 3: 1ch, dc in first st, work (2dc in next st, 1dc in next st) up to last st, 2dc in last st, join with a sl st in top of first dc. (15 sts)

Round 4: 1ch, dc in first 2 sts, work (2dc in next st, 1dc in next 2 sts) up to last 2 sts, 2dc in last st, join with a sl st in top of first dc. (20 sts)

Place st markers in first, 5th, 9th, 13th, and 17th sts.

Row 1 (RS): Join H in first marked st with a sl st, 1ch, 1dc in next 4sts, turn. (4 sts)

Row 2 (WS): 1ch, dc2tog, 1dc in next 2 sts, turn. (3 sts)

Row 3: 1ch, dc2tog, dc in next st, turn. (2 sts)

Row 4: 1ch, dc2tog, break off yarn.

Rep Rows 1–4 between marked sts 4 more times.

Next round: Join H in any st, 1ch, work 50dc evenly around outer edge of star, join with a sl st in top of first dc. (50 sts)

Next round: 1ch, dc in each st to end, join with a sl st in top of first dc. Break off yarn, leaving a long tail for sewing. Sew in ends.

Back

Make back in same way as front. Using long tail, sew front and back together using the whip stitch, stuffing as you work. Break off yarn. Sew in ends.

ASSEMBLY

Lay out a rain drop, cloud and rainbow for one strand, adjusting position until you are happy with each one. Cut a long strand of A and thread through each motif, knotting yarn at bottom and top of each motif to hold them into place. Repeat with two more rain drops, a cloud, and star, then with a star and a rainbow. Thread the sun on a short strand of yarn on its own.

Wrap each strand around the frame, adjusting length so each strand is a different length, and you achieve a fun, asymmetric effect. Secure the yarns tightly in place—add a small amount of super glue for extra security.

Climbing Colours Blanket

Bright colours climb a fluffy white background on this creative, reversible blanket. The combination of textures and colours will make this project a family favourite.

YOU WILL NEED

Aran weight
100% acrylic
(226 m/247 yd, 127 g/4.5 oz)

* 4 balls of white (A)
* I ball in the following colours:
* red (B), orange (C), yellow (D),
green (E), blue (F), purple (G)

EQUIPMENT

* 5.5 mm (US I/9) crochet hook
* Tapestry needle

TENSION

13 sts and 7 rows = 10 cm (4") in treble crochet

SIZE

78.5 x 109 cm (31 x 43")

SPECIAL STITCH

* Vst: (see page 10).

STRIPE SEQUENCE

Working with A for every Part A, change contrasting colours every Part B in this order: *B, C, D, E, F, then G; repeat from * for stripe sequence.

TO MAKE

Blanket

Foundation ch: With A, work 98ch.

Row 1: Beg in second ch from hook, work dc in each ch to end. (97 sts)

Row 2a: 3ch (counts as tr), 1tr in next st, 1ch, miss next 2 sts, 3tr in next st, *1ch, miss next 3 sts, 3tr in next st; repeat from * to last 4 sts, 1ch, miss next 2 sts, 1tr in last 2 sts.

(73 sts and 24 ch1sp)

Row 2b: 1ch, turn, dc in first st, change to B, work around sts from previous row, 1ch, miss next st, 1Vst in missed st below next ch, *1ch, miss next 3 sts, 1Vst in missed st below next ch; repeat from * to last 2 sts, 1ch, sl st in next st, miss last st. Break off B, but do not break off A.

(24 Vsts and 25 ch1sp)

Row 3a: Pick up A, work Stitch Pattern Part A.

Row 3b: With C, work Stitch Pattern Part B. Break off C, but not A.

Repeat rows 3a and 3b, continuing in Stripe Sequence, work Part B with D, E, F, G, then repeat entire sequence 8 more times. Break off all colours.

Sew in all ends.

Edging

Round 1: Do not turn. With A and top edge up, insert hook into first white st at beginning of previous row, yarn over hook and pull up a loop, 1ch, 1dc in

(MULTIPLE OF 4 STS + 1)

Part A: Do not turn. With white (A), insert hook into first (white) st at beginning of previous row, yarn over hook and pull up a loop, 1ch, 1htr in same st. Working into white sts from part A of the previous row, and around the coloured stitches from part B, tr in next st, *1ch, miss next Vst and next tr, 3tr in next tr, miss next tr; repeat from * to last Vst, 1ch, miss next Vst, 1tr in last 2 sts.

Part B: 1ch, turn, 1dc in first st and change to next contrasting colour (B–G) according to Stripe Sequence. Working around white sts from part A, 1ch, miss next st, 1Vst in centre of next Vst, * 1ch, miss next 3 sts, 1Vst in centre of next Vst; repeat from * up to last 2 sts, 1ch, sl st in next st, miss last st. Break off contrasting colour, but not A.

same st, 1htr in next white st, *1dc in centre of next Vst, miss next white tr, 3 tr in next white tr, miss next white tr; repeat from * to last Vst, dc in centre of last Vst, tr in last 2 white sts, rotate work with side edge at top, 1ch, work 135 dc evenly spaced across side edge, rotate work with foundation ch up, 1ch, dc in each ch across, rotate piece with remaining side edge up, 1ch, work 135 dc evenly spaced across side edge, join with a sl st in top of first dc. (464 sts and 4 ch1sp)

Join with sl st to first st.

Round 2: Turn, work (1sl st, 1ch) in each st and 1chsp around, join with a sl st in first st. Break off yarn. Sew in ends.

Mini Nesting Baskets

These nesting baskets are perfect for storing small items like cotton balls and hair bows. Make larger baskets by increasing the base and the sides by one round for each size.

YOU WILL NEED

Chunky weight
70% cotton/30% acrylic
(75 m/82 yd, 50 g/1.75 oz)

1 ball in the following colours:
raspberry (A), coral (B), lemon (C),
turquoise (D)

EQUIPMENT

* 4.5 mm (US 7) crochet hook
* 5 mm (US H/8) crochet hook
* Stitch marker
* Tapestry needle

TENSION

22 sts and 13 rounds = 10 cm (4")
in half treble crochet

SIZE

Small: 6.5 x 6 x 6.5 cm
(2½ x 2¼ x 2½")
Medium: 8 x 7 x 8 cm
(3¼ x 2¾ x 3¼")
Large: 9.5 x 7.5 x 9.5 cm
(3¾ x 3 x 3¾")
Extra Large: 11.75 x 8 x 11.75 cm
(4½ x 3¼ x 4½")

SPECIAL STITCHES

* FPdc (see page 112)

TURQUOISE BASKET

Base

With D and smaller crochet hook, make magic ring, leaving 10 cm (4") long tail.

Round 1: 2ch (throughout counts as htr), 9htr into ring, join with sl st in top of 2ch at beg of round. (10 sts)

Round 2: 2ch, 1htr in st at base of 2ch at beg of round, 2 htr in each st to end, join with a sl st in top of 2ch at beg of round. (20 sts)

Round 3: 2ch, 1htr in st at base of 2ch at beg of round, 1htr in next st, (2 htr in next st, 1htr in next st) 9 times, join with a sl st in top of 2ch at beg of round. (30 sts)

Round 4: 2ch, 1htr in st at base of 2ch at beg of round, htr in next 2 sts, (2htr in next st, 1htr in next 2 sts) 9 times, join with a sl st in top of 2ch at beg of round. (40 sts)

Round 5: 2ch, 1htr in st at base of 2ch at beg of round, 1htr in next 3 sts, (2htr in next st, 1htr in next 3 sts) 9 times, join with a sl st in top of 2ch at beg of round. (50 sts)

Round 6: 2ch, 1htr in st at base of 2ch at beg of round, 1htr in next 4 sts, (2htr in next st, 1htr in next 4 sts) 9 times, join with a sl st in top of 2ch at beg of round. (60 sts)

Round 7: 2ch, 1htr in st at base of 2ch at beg of round, 1htr in next 5 sts,

(2htr in next st, 1htr in next 5 sts) 9 times, join with a sl st in top of 2ch at beg of round. Break off yarn. (70 sts)

Sides

Change to larger crochet hook.

Round 1: Turn base with WS facing, join D with a FPdc around any st, FPdc in each st to end, join with a sl st in first FPdc, mark the sl st, turn. (70 sts)

Round 2: 1ch (does not count as st throughout), 1dc in marked sl st, 1ch, miss next st, *1dc in next st, 1ch, miss next st; rep from * to end, join with a sl st in first dc. (35 dc and 35 ch1sp)

Round 3: Sl st in next ch-1 sp, [ch 1, sc, ch 1] in same ch-1 sp, [sc, ch 1] in each ch-1 sp around, join with a sl st in first dc. (35 sts and 35 ch1sp)

Rounds 4–12: Repeat round 3.

Round 13: Sl st into next ch1sp, 4ch (counts as tr, 1ch), work (1tr, 1ch) in each ch1sp to end, join with a sl st in third ch of 4ch at beg of round. (35 tr and 35 ch1sp)

Round 14: 1ch, 2dc in each ch1sp to end, join with invisible join (see page 119). Break off yarn. (70 sts)

YELLOW BASKET

Base

With C, work base in same way as for Turquoise Basket up to round 6. Break off yarn. (60 sts)

Sides

Change to larger crochet hook.

Round 1: Turn base with WS facing, join C with a FPdc around any st, FPdc in each st around, join with a sl st in first FPdc, mark the sl st, turn. (60 sts)

Rounds 2–11: Work in same way as for Turquoise Basket. (30 dc and 30 ch1sp)

Round 12: Sl st into next ch1sp, 4ch (counts as tr, 1ch), work (1tr, 1ch) in each ch1sp to end, join with a sl st in third ch of 4ch at beg of round. (30 tr and 30 ch1sp)

Round 13: 1ch, 2dc in each ch1sp to end, join with invisible join. Break off yarn. (60 sts)

ORANGE BASKET

Base

With B, work base in same way as for Turquoise Basket up to round 5. Break off yarn. (50 sts)

Sides

Change to larger crochet hook.

Round 1: Turn base with WS facing, join B with a FPdc around any st, FPdc in each st around, join with a sl st in first FPdc, mark the sl st, turn. (50 sts)

Rounds 2–10: Work in same way as for Turquoise Basket. (25 dc and 25 ch1sp)

Round 11: Sl st into next ch1sp, 4ch (counts as tr, 1ch), work (1tr, 1ch) in each ch1sp to end, join with a sl st in third ch of 4ch at beg of round. (25 tr and 25 ch1sp)

Round 12: 1ch, 2dc in each ch1sp to end, join with invisible join. Break off yarn. (50 sts)

RED BASKET

Base

With A, work base in same way as for Turquoise Basket up to round 4. Break off yarn. (40 sts)

Sides

Change to larger crochet hook.

Round 1: Turn base with WS facing, join A with a FPdc around any st, FPdc in each st to end, join with a sl st in first FPdc, mark the sl st, turn. (40 sts)

Rounds 2–9: Work in same way as for Turquoise Basket. (20 dc and 20 ch1sp)

Round 10: Sl st into next ch1sp, 4ch (counts as tr, 1ch), work (1tr, 1ch) in each ch1sp to end, join with a sl st in third ch of 4ch at beg of round. (20 tr and 20 ch1sp)

Round 11: 1ch, 2dc in each ch1sp to end, join with invisible join. Break off yarn. (40 sts)

FINISHING

Weave in all ends.

Freddie Frog Bottle Cosy

Use a range of blue, purple, and green yarns to create a unique cosy
to cover your baby's milk bottle.

YOU WILL NEED

DK weight
60% cotton/40% acrylic
(140 m/153 yd, 50 g/1.75 oz)

∗ 1 ball in the following colours:
azure blue (A), lilac (B)
Small amounts in each of the
following colours:
lime green (C), grass green (D),
yellow (E), pink (F), white (G),
dark gray (H)

EQUIPMENT

∗ 3.5 mm (US E/4) crochet hook
∗ Stitch marker
∗ Tapestry needle

TENSION

16 sts and 8 rows = 10 cm (4") in
treble crochet

SIZE

Fits 20.5 cm (8") tall, 240ml (8 oz)
baby bottle with straight or angled
sides (not curved)

TO MAKE

Bottle Cozy

Foundation ring: With A, 5ch, join
with a sl st in first ch to form a ring (or
make a magic ring).
Round 1: 3ch (counts as tr), 11tr in
ring, join B and join last st with a sl st
in top of 3ch at beg of round; do not
fasten off A but leave at back of work.
(12 sts)
Round 2: With B, 3ch (counts as tr),
1tr in same st, 2tr in each st to end,
pick up A and join with a sl st in top of
3ch at beg of round,, leave B at back of
work. (24 sts)
Round 3: With A, 3ch, 1tr in same st,
1tr in next 5 sts, work (2tr in next st,

1tr in next 5 sts to end, pick up B and
join with a sl st in top of 3ch at beg of
round, leave A at back of work. (28 sts)
Round 4: With B, 3ch, 1tr in next st
and in each st to end, pick up A and
join with a sl st in top of 3ch at beg of
round, leave B at back of work.
Round 5: With A, 3ch, 1tr in next st
and in each st to end, pick up B and
join with a sl st in top of 3ch at beg of
round, leave A at back of work.
Rounds 6–14: Repeat rounds 4 and 5
four times, then repeat round 4 once
more. Break off both colours.

APPLIQUÉS

Lily Pad

Foundation ch: With D, work 16ch.
Row 1: Beg in fourth ch from hook,
work 4tr in same st, 1tr in next 11 ch,
5tr in last ch, rotate ch with opposite
side up, 1tr in next 11 ch, do not join.
Break off yarn.

Flower

Foundation ring: With E, 5ch, join with a sl st in first ch to form a ring (or make a magic ring).

Round 1: 1ch, 7dc in ring, join with a sl st in first dc. Break off yarn. (7 sts)

Round 2: Join F with a sl st in any dc, 1ch, 2tr in same st, 1ch, work (sl st in next dc, 2tr in next st, 1ch) to end, join with a sl st in first sl st. Break off yarn. (7 petals)

Frog

Foundation ring: With C, 5ch, join with a sl st in first ch to form a ring (or make a magic ring).

Round 1: 1ch, 8dc in ring, do not join; work rounds in a spiral, place marker to mark beg of rounds. (8 sts)

Round 2: 2dc in each st around. (16 sts)

Round 3: (2dc in next st, 1dc in next st) to end. (24 sts)

Round 4: Miss next st, 7dtr in next st, miss next st, 1dc in next st, miss next st, 7dtr in next st, miss next st, 1dc in next 3 sts, work (3dtr, 4ch, sl st) into next st, 1dc in next 9 sts, work (sl at, 4ch, 3dtr) in next st, 1dc in next 2 sts, sl st in next st.
Break off yarn.

Eyes (make 2)

Round 1: With H, 2ch, work 6dc in second ch from hook, join with a sl st in first dc. Break off yarn. (6 sts)

Round 2: Join G with dc in any st, 1dc in same st, 2dc in each st around, join with a sl st in first dc. Break off yarn. (12 sts)

Sew eyes to 7dtr shells at top of frog, with green showing around eyes as shown in photo.

FINISHING

Weave in ends on all pieces.

Bottle Cosy Drawstring

With D, work 50ch. Break off yarn, leaving a small tail.

Thread drawstring through stitches of last round of cosy.

Cut 4 pieces of D, each 10 cm (4") long for tassels. Holding 2 pieces together, fold in half and pull loop through end st of chain, then pull all ends through loop. Pull snug and trim all ends to 2.5 cm (1"). Repeat with remaining 2 pieces of D on other end of chain. Tie bow snugly around neck of bottle.

Sew lily pad to bottle cosy, then frog on top of lily pad, using photo as reference. Sew flower to bottle cosy, sewing around center and leaving petals free. Slip cosy over bottle.

Monster Cushion Cover

Creative and easy to make, this Monster Cushion Cover can also be used to store toys and baby clothes. The simple back flap makes it easy to remove the cushion for cleaning.

YOU WILL NEED

Chunky weight
70% cotton/30% acrylic
(75 m/82 yd, 50 g/1.75 oz)

* 2 balls of sky blue (A)
* 1 ball in the following colours:
grass green (B), coral (C),
lemon yellow (D), white (E)

EQUIPMENT

* 4.5 mm (US 7) crochet hook
* Stitch marker
* Two small circles of felt in black
or dark brown
* Embroidery thread in black or
dark brown
* Tapestry needle

TENSION

13½ sts and 10 rows = 10 cm (4")
in pattern

SIZE

30 x 40 cm (11¾ x 15¾")

TO MAKE

Ears (make 1 in C and 1 in D)

Round 1: Make a magic ring, 1ch, 6dc into ring, do not join. (6 sts)

Round 2: 2dc in each st to end, do not join. (12 sts)

Round 3: *1dc in next st, 2dc in next st; repeat from * 5 more times, do not join. (18 sts)

Rounds 4–7: 1dc in each st to end, sl st in next st of last round. Break off yarn. Sew in ends.

Legs (make 2)

Round 1: With A, make a magic ring, 1ch (does not count as a st), 6dc into ring, do not join. (6 sts)

Round 2: 2dc in each st to end, do not join. (12 sts)

Round 3: *1dc in next st, 2dc in next st; repeat from * 5 more times, do not join. (18 sts)

Rounds 4–13: 1dc in each st to end, sl st in next st of last round. Break off yarn. Sew in ends.

Body

Body begins at the top of the back and works down to the bottom when the legs are joined. Work then continues up the front, when the ears are joined on the last row of the front.

Foundation ch: With E, work 41ch.

Row 1 (WS): Beg in second ch from hook, 1dc in each ch to end, turn. (40 sts)

Row 2 (RS): 2ch (does not count as a st), 1tr in each st to end, turn.

Row 3: 1ch (does not count as st), 1dc in each st to the end, turn.

Row 4: Repeat row 2, changing to B at end of row.

Rows 5–8: With B, work in established patt, changing to D at end of last row.

Rows 9–12: With D, work in etablished patt, changing to C at end of last row.

Rows 13–16: With C, work in established patt, changing to E at end of last row.

Rows 17–20: With E, work in established patt, changing to B at end of last row.

Rows 21–24: With B, work in established patt, changing to D at end of last row.

Rows 25–28: With D, work in established patt, changing to C at end of last row.

Row 29: With C, 1ch, 1dc in first 5 sts, holding first leg behind body and with top edges held together, work 1dc in next 9 sts, working through all 3 layers, 1dc in next 12 sts, hold second leg behind body same as first leg and 1dc in next 9 sts, 1dc to end, turn.

Rows 30–32: With C, work in established patt, changing to E at end of last row.

Rows 33–36: With E, work in established patt, changing to B at end of last row.

Rows 37–40: With B, work in established patt, changing to D at end of last row.

Rows 41–44: With D, work in established patt, changing to C at end of last row.

Rows 45–48: With C, work in established patt, changing to A at end of last row.

Rows 49–68: With A, work in established patt.

Row 69: With A, 1ch, holding first ear behind body and with top edges held together, work 1dc in first 9 sts working through all 3 layers, 1dc in next 22 sts, hold second ear behind body same as first ear and 1dc in next 9 sts same as first ear, turn.

Rows 70–89: With A, work in established patt. Break off yarn. Sew in all ends.

Big Eye (make 1)

Foundation: With E, make a magic ring.

Round 1: 1ch (does not count as a st), 6dc into ring, do not join. (6 sts)

Round 2: 2dc in each st around, do not join. (12 sts)

Round 3: *1dc in next st, 2dc in next st; repeat from * 5 more times, do not join. (18 sts)

Round 4: *2dc in next st, 1dc in each of next 2 sts; repeat from * 5 more times, do not join. (24 sts)

Round 5: *1dc in each of next 3 sts, 2dc in next st; repeat from * 5 more times, do not join. (30 sts)

Round 6: *1dc in next st, 2dc in next st, 1dc in each of next 3 sts; repeat from * 5 more times, do not join. (36 sts)

Round 7: *1dc in each of next 3 sts, 2dc in next st, 1dc in each of next 2 sts; repeat from * 5 more times, join with a sl st in next st. Break off yarn. (42 sts)

Small Eye (make 1)

Rounds 1–5: Make in same way as for Big Eye, sl st in next st at end of last round. Break off yarn. (30 sts)

Arms (make 1 in B and 1 in D)

Foundation: Make a magic ring.

Round 1: 1ch (does not count as a st), 6dc into ring, do not join. (6 sts)

Round 2: 2dc in each st around, do not join. (12 sts)

Rounds 3–7: 1dc in each st around, do not join.

Round 8: *1dc in next st, dc2tog; repeat from * 3 more times, do no join. (8 sts remain)

Rounds 9–20: 1dc in each st around, join with a sl st in next st of last round. Break off yarn. Sew in ends.

FINISHING

Pin eyes to front of head, and with B threaded in tapestry needle, sew eyes to head using running st. Sew circles of felt onto each eye using blanket stitch. Embroider mouth with C. Fold body at rows 29 and 69 with RS on outside, and top of back overlapping the lower part.

With C, join each side edge by working a row of dc through all layers. Break off yarn. Sew arms to body.

Fun Shapes Organiser

Whether it's toys or toiletries, this organiser is a great place to keep all of your baby's belongings, as well as brightening up the nursery!

YOU WILL NEED

Aran weight
100% cotton
(80 m/87 yd, 50 g/1.75 oz)

* 4 balls of turquoise (A)
* 1 ball in the following colours:
lime green (B), orange (C), red (D),
light gray (E), bright yellow (F)

EQUIPMENT

* 5 mm (US H/8) crochet hook
* Stitch marker
* Three 25 mm (1") buttons
* Hanger measuring about 38 cm
(15") across bottom

TENSION

15 sts and 17 rows = 10 cm (4") in
double crochet

SIZE

37.5 x 44.5 cm (14¾ x 17½"), with
top folded over.

TO MAKE

Main Panel

Foundation ch: With A, work 56ch.
Row 1: Beg in dc in second ch from hook, 1dc in each ch to end, turn. (55 sts)
Row 2: 1ch, 1dc in each dc to end, turn.
  Repeat last row until piece measures approximately 45 cm (17¾").
Buttonhole row: 1ch, 1dc in first 8 sts, work (3ch, miss next 3 sts, 1dc in next 15 sts) 2 times, 3ch, miss next 3 sts, 1dc in last 8 sts, turn.
  Repeat row 2 three more times. Break off yarn. Sew in ends.

Top Pockets

Foundation ch: With C, work 17ch.
Row 1: Beg in second ch from hook, 1dc in each ch to end, turn. (16 sts)
Row 2: 1ch, 1dc in each st to end, turn.
Rows 3–18: Repeat row 2, then break off yarn at end of last row.
Row 19: Join B with 1dc in first st, 1dc in each st to end, turn.
Rows 20–40: Repeat row 2, then break off yarn at end of last row.
Row 41: Join D with 1dc in first st, 1dc in each st to end, turn.
Rows 42–58: Repeat row 2, then break off yarn at end of last row.
  Sew in ends.

Bottom Pockets

Foundation ch: With E, work 24ch.
Row 1: Beg in dc in second ch from hook and 1dc in each ch to end, turn. (23 sts)
Row 2: 1ch, 1dc in each st to end, turn.
Rows 3–18: Repeat row 2, then break

off yarn at end of last row.

Row 19: Join F with dc in first st, 1dc in each st to end, turn.

Rows 20–40: Repeat row 2, then break off yarn at end of last row.

Row 41: Join B with dc in first st, 1dc in each st to end, turn.

Rows 42–58: Repeat row 2, then break off yarn at end of last row.

Sew in ends.

Geometric Pieces

Circle (make 1 in D and 1 in E)

Foundation round: 5ch, join with a sl st in first ch to form ring (or make a magic ring).

Round 1: 1ch, 8dc in ring, do not join; work rounds in a spiral, place marker to mark beginning of round. (8 sts)

Round 2: 2dc in each st to end. (16 sts)

Round 3: Work (2dc in next st, 1dc in next st) to end join with a sl st in next st. (24 sts)

Break off yarn, leaving a long tail for sewing.

Long Vertical Rectangle (make 1 in F and 1 in B)

Foundation ch: Work 7ch.

Row 1: Beg in second ch from hook, 1dc in each ch to end, turn. (6 sts)

Row 2: 1ch, 1dc in each st to end, turn.

Rows 3–12: Repeat row 2, then break off yarn at end of last row, leaving a long tail for sewing.

Small Square (make 1 in D)

Foundation ch: Work 7ch.

Row 1: Beg in second ch from hook and 1dc in each ch to end, turn. (6 sts)

Row 2: 1ch, 1dc in each st to end, turn.

Rows 3–6: Repeat row 2, then break off yarn at end of last row, leaving a long tail for sewing.

Medium Square (make 2 in C)

Foundation ch: Work 9ch.

Row 1: Beg in second ch from hook and 1dc in each ch to end, turn. (8 sts)

Row 2: 1ch, 1dc in each st across, turn.

Rows 3–8: Repeat row 2, then break off yarn at end of last row, leaving a long tail for sewing.

Large Square (make 1 in A)

Foundation ch: Work 11ch.

Row 1: Beg in second ch from hook and 1dc in each ch to end, turn. (10 sts)

Row 2: 1ch, 1dc in each st to end, turn.

Rows 3–10: Repeat row 2, then break off yarn at end of last row, leaving a long tail for sewing.

Long Horizontal Rectangle (make 1 in A)

Foundation ch: Work 13ch.

Row 1: Beg in second ch from hook and 1dc in each ch to end, turn. (12 sts)

Row 2: 1ch, 1dc in each st to end, turn.

Rows 3–6: Repeat row 2, then break off yarn at end of last row, leaving a long tail for sewing.

Small Vertical Rectangle (make 1 in E)

Foundation row: Work 5ch.

Row 1: Beg in second ch from hook and 1dc in each ch to end, turn. (4 sts)

Row 2: 1ch, 1dc in each st to end, turn.

Rows 3–8: Repeat row 2, then break off yarn at end of last row, leaving a long tail for sewing.

FINISHING

Sew in beginning tails of each geometric piece.

Block main panel to 37.5 cm (14¾") *wide and 47.5 cm (18¾") long, top pocket to 11 cm (4¼") wide and 35 cm (13¾") long, and bottom pocket to 16 cm (6¼") wide and 35 cm (13¾") long (see page 121).

Place each geometric piece on both pockets, using photo as a guide. Sew each piece to pocket using the long tails.

Pin both pockets to main panel as shown in photo. With D and RS facing, begin at top of bottom pocket, join pocket to main panel with sl st through both layers along sides and bottom, then continuing sl st around remaining edges, joining sides of top pocket as you work. Break off yarn.

With D and RS facing, join bottom edge of top pocket using sl st along bottom edge. Break off yarn.

With D and RS facing, sl st along colour divisions of each pocket to form smaller pockets. Break off yarn at end of each pocket seam.

Sew buttons to RS, 15 rows from top edge. Button top edge over hanger.

Drops Storage Basket

Form meets function in this sturdy storage basket. The top can be rolled down for added stability, or use the handles for easy, one handed carry.

YOU WILL NEED

Chunky weight
100% acrylic
(132 m/114 yd, 220 g/7.76 oz)

* 3 balls of light blue (A)
* 1 ball of charcoal (B)
* Small amounts in the
following colours:
red (C), yellow (D), green (E),
blue (F), purple (G)

EQUIPMENT

* 10 mm (US N/P/15) crochet
hook
* Tapestry needle

TENSION

7 sts and 6 rows = 10 cm (4") in
treble crochet

SIZE

30 x 30 x 30 cm
(11¾ × 11¾ × 11¾")

SPECIAL STITCHES

* FPdtr (see page 112)
* BPhtr (see page 112)

TO MAKE

Base

Foundation ring: With 2 strands of B held together, make a magic ring, leaving a 10 cm (4") tail.

Round 1: 3ch (counts as 1tr), 1tr, 1dtr, work (2tr, 1dtr) 3 times, join with a sl st in top of 3ch at beg of round, sl st in next tr and dtr. (12 sts)

Round 2: 3ch (counts as tr throughout), work (1tr, 1dtr, 1tr) in st at base of 3ch at beg of round, 1tr in next 2 sts, * work (2tr, 1dtr, 2tr) in next st, 1tr in next 2 sts; rep from * to end,

join with a sl st in top of 3ch at beg of round, sl st in next tr and dtr. (28 sts)

Round 3: 3ch, work (1tr, 2dtr, 2tr) in st at base of 3ch as beg of round, 1tr in next 6sts, * work (2tr, 1dtr, 2tr) in next st, 1tr in next 6sts; rep from * to end, join with a sl st in top of 3ch at beg of round, sl st in next tr and dtr. (44 sts)

Round 4: 3ch, work (1tr, 1dtr, 2tr) in st at base of 3ch at beg of round, 1tr in next 10sts, * work (2tr, 1dtr, 2tr) in next st, 1tr in next 10sts; rep from * to end, join with a sl st in top of 3ch at beg of round, sl st in next tr and dtr. (60 sts)

Round 5: 3ch, work (1tr, 1dtr, 2tr) in st at base of 3ch at beg of round, 1tr in next 14sts, * work (2tr, 1dtr, 2tr) in next st, 1tr in next 14sts; rep from * to end, join with a sl st in top of 3ch at beg of round, sl st in next tr and dtr. (76 sts)

Round 6: 3ch, work (1tr, 1dtr, 2tr) in st at base of 3ch at beg of round, 1tr in nest 18sts, * work (2tr, 1dtr, 2tr) in

next st, 1tr in next 18sts; rep from * to end, join with a sl st in top of 3ch at beg of round. (92 sts)

Break off yarn. Sew in ends.

Sides

Round 1: With 2 strands of A held together and RS facing, join yarn with a sl st around the back post of any corner dtr, 2ch (counts as htr throughout), BPhtr in each st to end, join with a sl st in top of 2ch at beg of round. (92 sts)

Round 2: Sl st in next 2 sts, 2ch, 1htr in next 20 sts, miss next 2sts, *1htr in next 21sts, miss next 2sts; rep from * 2 more times, join with a sl st in top of 2ch at beg of round. (84 sts)

Round 3: Sl st in next st, 2ch, 1htr in next 19 sts, FPdtr around first missed st from round 1, miss next st of round 2, *1htr in next 20 sts, FPdtr around first missed st from round 1, miss next st of round 2; rep from * 2 more times, join with a sl st in top of 2ch at beg of round. (84 st)

Round 4: 2ch, 1htr in each st to end, join with a sl st in top of 2ch at beg of round.

Round 5: Sl st in next st, 2ch, 1htr in next 19 sts, 1FPdtr around FPdtr 2 rounds below, miss next st of previous round, *1htr in next 20 sts, 1FPdtr around FPdtr 2 rounds below, miss next st of previous round; rep from * 2 more times, join with a sl st in top of 2ch at beg of round.

Rounds 6–13: Repeat rounds 4 and 5 four more times.

Round 14: Repeat round 4.

Round 15: Sl st in next st, 2ch, 1htr in next 6 sts, 6ch, miss next 6 sts, 1htr in next 7 sts, 1FPdtr around FPdtr 2 rounds below, miss next st of previous round, 1htr in next 20 sts, 1FPdtr around FPdtr 2 rounds below, miss next st of previous round, 1htr in next 7 sts, 6ch, miss next 6 sts, 1htr in next 7 sts, 1FPdtr around FPdtr 2 rounds below, miss next st of previous round, 1htr in next 20 sts, 1FPdtr around FPdtr 2 rounds below, miss next st of

previous round, join with a sl st in top of 2ch at beg of round. (72 sts and 2 ch6sp)

Round 16: 2ch, 1htr in next 6 sts, 6htr in ch6sp, 1htr in next 36 sts, 6htr in ch6sp, 1htr in next 29 sts, join with a sl st in top of 2ch at beg of round. (84 sts)

Round 17: Repeat round 5. Break off yarn.

FINISHING

Sew in ends.

Rainbow Waves Buggy Blanket

This beautiful, rainbow blanket, with its front post stitches, will keep your little one cosy and protected from the cold.

YOU WILL NEED

Aran weight
50% merino wool/25% acrylic/
25% microfibre
(105 m/115 yd, 50 g/1.75 oz)

2 balls of orange (G), yellow (H)
∗ 1 ball in the following colours:
purple (A), off white (B), red (C),
turquoise (D), bright green (E),
cyan (F)

EQUIPMENT

∗ 4 mm (US G/6) crochet hook
∗ Stitch marker
∗ Tapestry needle

TENSION

18 sts and 19 rows = 10 cm (4") in
alternating rows of double crochet
and half treble crochet

SIZE

71 x 61 cm (28 x 24")

SPECIAL STITCHES

FPdtr (see page 112)

STRIPE SEQUENCE

10 rows with A, 1 row with B, 11 rows with C, 1 row with B, 13 rows with D, 1 row with B, 13 rows with E, 1 row with B, 2 rows with A, 13 rows with F, 1 row with B, 17 rows with G, 1 row with B, 2 rows with C, 9 rows with H, 1 row with B, 7 rows with G, 1 row with B, then 10 rows with H.

WORKING THE LOOPS

All double crochets (dc) used in the main blanket pattern are worked under 3 loops of htr.

TO MAKE

Foundation ch: With A, work 126ch.
Row 1 (WS): Beg in third ch from hook (missed ch do not count as a st), 1htr in each ch across, turn. (124 sts)
Row 2 (RS): 1ch (does not count as a st), 1dc in first 4 sts, *1FPdtr in same st as last dc, miss next st in previous row, 1dc in next 5 sts, 1FPdtr around last st of previous row worked, 1FPdtr around next st in previous row (the st below last FPdtr), miss 2 sts in previous row behind the 2 FPdtr, 1dc in next 7 sts; rep from * 7 more times, turn.
Row 3 (WS): 2ch (does not count as a st), 1htr in each st to end, turn.
Row 4: 1ch, 1dc in first 5 sts, *1FPdtr around FPdtr 2 rows below, miss next st of previous row, 1dc in next 5 sts, 1FPdtr around each of 2 FPdtr 2 rows below, miss 2 sts in previous row**, 1dc in next 7 sts; rep from * 6 more times, then from * to ** once, 1dc in last 6 sts, turn.
Row 5: Repeat row 3.

Row 6: 1ch, 1dc in first 6 sts, *1FPdtr around FPdtr 2 rows below, miss next st of previous row, 1dc in next 5 sts, 1FPdtr around each of 2 FPdtr 2 rows below, miss next 2 sts of previous row**, 1dc into next 7 sts; rep from * 6 more times, then rep from * to ** once, 1dc in last 5 sts, turn.

Row 7: Repeat row 3.

Row 8: 1ch, 1dc in first 7 sts, *1FPdtr around FPdtr 2 rows below, miss next st of previous row, 1dc in next 5 sts, 1FPdtr around each of 2 FPdtr 2 rows below, miss next 2 sts of previous row**, 1dc in next 7 sts; rep from * 6 more times, then from * to ** once, 1dc in last 4 sts, turn.

Row 9: Repeat row 3.

Row 10: Repeat row 8.

Row 11: With B, repeat row 3.

Row 12: With C, repeat row 6.

Row 13: Repeat row 3.

Row 14: Repeat row 4.

Row 15: Repeat row 3.

Row 16: 1ch, 1dc in first 4 sts, *1FPdtr around FPdtr 2 rows below, miss next st of previous row, 1dc in next 5 sts, 1FPdtr around each of 2 FPdtr from 2 rows below, miss next 2 sts of previous row, 1dc in next 7 sts; rep from * 7 more times, turn.

Row 17: Repeat row 3.

Row 18: Repeat row 16.

Row 19: Repeat row 3.

Rows 20–115: Repeat rows 4–19

six more times, working colours in established Stripe Sequence. Do not break off yarn after last row, turn.

Edging

Round 1: With RS facing, 1ch, 3dc in first st, 1dc in next 122 sts, 3dc in last st to turn corner, work 115dc evenly spaced along side edge (1dc in each row), 3dc in first ch of foundation ch to turn corner, 1dc in next 122ch, 3dc in last ch to turn corner, 115dc evenly spaced along remaining side edge, join with a sl st in first dc. Break off yarn.

Round 2 (RS): Join B with a sl st in any st along edge, 1ch, working from left to right, *insert hook in st to right of hook, yoh and draw through a loop, yoh and draw through both loops on hook; repeat from * to end, join with a sl st in top of first reverse dc. Break off yarn.

FINISHING

Sew in all ends and block.

COLOUR CHANGE

When changing colours for the next row, work the last yoh of the last stitch of the row with the new colour for a smooth transition.

Buddy Bear Curtain Tie

This little bear will brighten up any nursery! Use fun colours to complement or contrast with your room design.

YOU WILL NEED

DK weight
50% cotton/50% polyester
(105 m/115 yd, 50 g/1.75 oz)

* 1 ball in the following colours:
pale lilac (A), light purple (B),
bright pink (C), light pink (D),
cream (E), bright purple (F)

EQUIPMENT

* 3.25 mm (US D/3) crochet hook
* 2 × small safety eyes
* 1 × 15 mm (¾") button
* Polyester stuffing

TENSION

24 sts and 24 rounds = 10 cm (4")
in double crochet

SIZE

Head circumference: 23 cm (9")
Length: 18 cm (7")

TO MAKE

Head

With A, make a magic ring.

Round 1: 1ch in ring, work 6dc in ring, join with a sl st in top of first dc. (6 sts)

Round 2: 1ch, 2dc in each st to end, join with a sl st in top of first dc. Break off A. (12 sts)

Round 3: Join B with a sl st, 1ch, 1dc in first st, work (2dc in next st, 1dc in next st) up to last st, 2dc in last st, join with a sl st in top of first dc. (18 sts)

Round 4: 1ch, 1dc in first 2 sts, work (2dc in next st, 1dc in next st) up to last st, 2dc in last st, join with a sl st in top of first dc. Break off yarn. (24 sts)

Round 5: Join C with a sl st, 1ch, 1dc in first 3 sts, work (2dc in next st, 1dc in next st) up to last st, 2dc in last st, join with a sl st in top of first dc. (30 sts)

Round 6: 1ch, 1dc in first 4 sts, work (2dc in next st, 1dc in next 4sts) up to last st, 2dc in last st, join with a sl st in top of first dc. Break off C. (36 sts)

Round 7: Join D with a sl st, 1ch, 1dc in first 5 sts, work (2dc in next st, 1dc in next 5 sts) up to last st, 2dc in last st, join with a sl st in top of first dc. (42 sts)

Round 8: 1ch, 1dc in first 6 sts, work (2dc in next st, 1dc in next 6 sts) up to last st, 2dc in last st, join with a sl st in top of first dc. Break off D. (48 sts)

Round 9: Join E with a sl st, 1ch, 1dc in first 7 sts, work (2dc in next st, 1dc in next 7 sts) last st, join with a sl st in top of first dc. (54 sts)

Round 10: 1ch, 1dc in each st to end, join with a sl st in top of first dc. Break off E.

Rounds 11 and 12: Join F with a sl st,

1ch, 1dc in each st to end, join with a sl st in top of first dc. Break off yarn at end of round 12.

Round 13: Join A with a sl st, 1ch, 1dc in each st around, join with a sl st in top of first dc.

Round 14: 1ch, 1dc in first 22 sts, 1ch, miss next st, 1dc in next 9 sts, 1ch, miss next st, 1dc in each st to end of round, join with a sl st in top of first dc. Break off A.

Round 15: Join B with a sl st, 1ch, 1dc in each st and ch1sp to end, join with a sl st in top of first dc.

Round 16: 1ch, 1dc in each st to end, join with a sl st in top of first dc. Break off B.

Rounds 17 and 18: Join C with a sl st, 1ch, 1dc in each st to end, join with a sl st in top of first dc. Break off yarn at end of round 18.

Round 19: Join D with a sl st, 1ch, 1dc in first 7 sts, work (dc2tog, 1dc in next 7 sts) up to last 2 sts, dc2tog, join with a sl st in top of first dc. (48 sts)

Round 20: 1ch, 1dc in first 6 sts, work (dc2tog, 1dc in next 6 sts) up to last 2 sts, dc2tog, join with a sl st in top of first dc. Break off D. (42 sts)

Round 21: Join E with a sl st, 1ch, 1dc in first 5 sts, work (dc2tog, 1dc in next 5 sts) up to last 2 sts, dc2tog, join with a sl st in top of first dc. (36 sts)

Round 22: 1ch, 1dc in first 4 sts, work (dc2tog, 1dc in next 4 sts) up to last

2 sts, dc2tog, join with a sl st in top of first dc. Break off E. (30 sts)

Insert eyes into holes in Round 14 following manufacturer's instructions. Beg stuffing head now, and add additional stuffing as you work.

Round 23: Join F with a sl st, 1ch, 1dc in first 3 sts, work (dc2tog, 1dc in next 3 sts) up to last 2 sts, dc2tog, join with a sl st in top of first dc. (24 sts)

Round 24: 1ch, 1dc in first 2 sts, work (dc2tog, 1dc in next 2 sts) up to last 2 sts, dc2tog, join with a sl st in top of first dc. Break off F. (18 sts)

Round 25: Join A with a sl st, 1ch, 1dc in first st, work (dc2tog, 1dc in next st) up to last 2 sts, dc2tog, join with a sl st in top of first dc. (12 sts)

Round 26: 1ch, work(dc2tog) to end, join with a sl st in top of first st. Break off A, leaving a long tail. (6 sts)

Thread tail through tops of remaining sts, then pull tight to close hole. Break off.

Muzzle

Foundation ch: With A, work 3ch.

Round 1: Beg in second ch from hook, work 5dc in each of next 2ch, join with a sl st in top of first dc. (10 sts)

Round 2: 1ch, 1dc in first 2 sts, 2dc in each of next 3 sts, 1dc in next 2 sts, 2dc in next 3 sts, join with a sl st in top of first dc. (16 sts)

Round 3: 1ch, 1dc in first 5 sts, 2dc in next st, 1dc in next 7 sts, 2dc in next st, 1dc in next 2 sts, join with a sl st in top of first dc. (18 sts)

Round 4: 1ch, 1dc in first 5 sts, 2dc in each of next 2 sts, 1dc in next 7 sts, 2dc in each of next 2 sts, 1dc in next 2 sts, join with a sl st in top of dc. (20 sts)

Break off, leaving a tail for sewing. Begin sewing muzzle to head as shown in photo and lightly fill with stuffing as you work. Embroider nose and mouth with F, using straight and satin sts.

Body

With A, make a magic ring.

Rounds 1–7: Work same as for head. (42 sts)

Round 8: 1ch, 1dc in each st to end, join with a sl st in top of first dc. Break off D.

Rounds 9 and 10: Join E with a sl st, 1ch, 1dc in each st to end, join with a sl st in top of first dc. Break off E at end of round 10.

Round 11: Join F with a sl st, 1ch, 1dc in first 5 sts, work (dc2tog, 1dc in next 5 sts) up to last 2 sts, dc2tog, join with a sl st in top of first dc. (36 sts)

Round 12: 1ch, 1dc in each st to end, join with a sl st in top of first dc. Break off F.

Round 13: Join A with a sl st, 1ch, 1dc in first 4 sts, work (dc2tog, 1dc in next 4 sts) up to last 2 sts, dc2tog, join with a sl st in top of first dc. (30 sts)

Round 14: 1ch, 1dc in each st around, join with a sl st in top of first dc. Break off A.

Rounds 15 and 16: Join B with a sl st, 1ch, 1dc in each st to end, join with a sl st in top of first dc. Break off B at end of round 16. Beg stuffing head now, and add additional stuffing as you work.

Round 17: Join C with a sl st, 1ch, 1dc in first 3 sts, work (dc2tog, 1dc in next 3 sts) up to last 2 sts, dc2tog, join with a sl st in top of first dc. (24 sts)

Round 18: 1ch, 1dc in first 2 sts, work (dc2tog, 1dc in next 2 sts) up to last 2 sts, dc2tog, join with a sl st in top of first dc. Break off C. (18 sts)

Round 19: Join D with a sl st, 1ch, 1dc in first st, work (dc2tog, 1dc in next st) up to last 2 sts dc2tog, join with a sl st in top of first dc. Break off D, leaving a long tail. (12 sts)

Complete stuffing body then sew it to head.

Ears (make 2)

With A, make a magic ring.

Row 1: 1ch in ring, work 6dc in ring, 1ch and turn. Do not join (6 sts)

Row 2: 1dc in first st, work (2dc in next st, 1dc in next st) up to last st, 2dc in last st. Break off, leaving a long tail. (9 sts)

Sew ears to head.

Legs (make 2)

With A, make a magic ring.

Round 1: 1ch in ring, work 6dc in ring, join with a sl st in top of first dc. (6 sts)

Round 2: 1ch, 2dc in each st to end, join with a sl st in top of first dc. Break off A. (12 sts)

Round 3: Join B with a sl st, 1ch, 1dc in first st, work (2dc in next st, 1dc in next st) up to last st, 2dc in last st, join with a sl st in top of first dc. (18 sts)

Round 4: 1ch, 1dc in each st to end, join with a sl st in top of first dc. Break off B.

Round 5: Join C with a sl st, 1ch, 1dc in first 2 sts, work (2dc in next st, 1dc in next 2 sts) up to last st, 2dc in last st, join with a sl st in top of first dc. (24 sts)

Round 6: 1ch, 1dc in each st to end, join with a sl st in top of first dc. Break off C.

Rounds 7 and 8: Join D with a sl st, 1ch, 1dc in each st to end, join with a sl st in top of first dc. Break off D at end of round 8.

Round 9: Join E with a sl st, 1ch, 1dc in first 6 sts, work (dc2tog, 1dc in next 6 sts) up to last 2 sts, dc2tog, join with a sl st in top of first dc. (21 sts)

Round 10: 1ch, 1dc in first 5 sts, work (dc2tog, 1dc in next 5 sts) up to last 2 sts, dc2tog, join with a sl st in top of first dc. Break off E, leaving a long tail.

Lightly stuff legs. Sew legs to body.

Arms (make 2)

With A, make a magic ring.

Round 1: 1ch in ring, work 6dc in ring, join with a sl st in top of first dc. (6 sts)

Round 2: 1ch, 2dc in each st to end, join with a sl st in top of first dc. Break off A. (12 sts)

Rounds 3 and 4: Join B with a sl st, 1ch, 1dc in each st to end, join with a sl st in top of first dc. Break off B at end of round 4.

Rounds 5 and 6: Join C with a sl st, 1ch, 1dc in each st to end, join with a sl st in top of first dc. Break off C at end of round 6.

Rounds 7 and 8: Join D with a sl st, 1ch, 1dc in each st to end, join with a sl st in top of first dc. Break off D at end of round 8, leaving a long tail.

Lightly stuff arms. Sew arms to body.

Tail

With A, make a magic ring.

Round 1: 1ch in round, work 8dc in ring, join with a sl st in top of first dc. (8 sts)

Round 2: 1ch, work (dc2tog) 4 times, join with a sl st in top of first dc. Break off, leaving a tail.

Lightly stuff tail. Sew tail to body.

Right Strap

Foundation ch: With B, work 5ch.

Row 1: Beg in second ch from hook, work 1htr in each ch to end. Break off, leaving a long tail. (4 sts)

Sew button on one end of strap, and sew other end of strap to right arm.

Left Strap

Foundation ch: With B, work 25ch.

Row 1: Beg in eighth ch from hook (to create buttonhole), work 1dc in next 18ch, 1ch and turn. (18 sts)

Row 2: Sl st in next 18 sts, work 8dc around buttonhole, continue along other edge, sl st in in each st to end. Break off, leaving a long tail. (44 sts)

TO FINISH

Sew end of strap without buttonhole to left arm. Sew in any remaining ends.

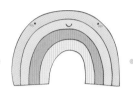

TECHNIQUES

Tools and Materials

YARN

Before you start a project, you will need to decide which type of yarn you would like to use: animal, plant, or synthetic. Each type of yarn fibre has its own unique characteristics. Wool, for instance (animal), is warm and absorbent but requires careful washing and drying. Cotton, bamboo, hemp, and linen (plant) are lightweight and breathe well. They are easier to wash and work well for warm-weather garments. Synthetic fibres, like acrylic and polyester, are the cheapest of the yarn options. They are machine washable, making them the most popular choice for beginners.

Yarn also comes in various different weights (or 'thicknesses') and the names for these weights differs from country to country. To make sure that you are using the correct yarn weight, check the ball band of your yarn for a recommended hook size and tension, and compare that to the tension specified in the pattern. Working up a tension swatch is also a good idea.

YARN WEIGHTS

Yarn-weight symbol and category name	Super Fine	Fine	Light	Medium	Bulky	Super Bulky
Types of yarn in category	Sock, Fingering, Baby	Sport, Baby	DK, Light, Worsted	Worsted, Afghan, Aran	Chunky, Craft, Rug	Bulky, Roving
Crochet tension ranges* in Double Crochet to 10 cm	21 to 32 sts	16 to 20 sts	12 to 17 sts	11 to 14 sts	8 to 11 sts	5 to 9 sts
Recommended hook in metric size range	2.25 to 3.5 mm	3.5 to 4.5 mm	4.5 to 5.5 mm	5.5 to 6.5 mm	6.5 to 9 mm	9 mm and larger
Recommended hook in US size range	B/1 to E/4	E/4 to 7	7 to I/9	I/9 to K/10½	K/10½ to M/13	M/13 and larger

*These are guidelines only. They reflect the most commonly used tensions and needles or hook sizes for specific yarn categories.

CROCHET HOOKS

Crochet hooks are available in many different materials, shapes, and sizes. Depending on your grip (see Holding Your Hook, page 104), you might find one type of hook more comfortable than another. Ergonomic hooks, for example, are great for people who have wrist pain.

Keep in mind that some materials work better with specific yarns. Wooden hooks work well with slippery yarns, like Merino, but not so well with acrylics or synthetic yarns.

Some hooks also have blunter tips than others, making them better to use with yarn that splits, such as cotton.

SCISSORS, TAPESTRY NEEDLE, STITCH MARKERS, AND PINS

A small pair of scissors with sharp blades should be used to cut your yarn ends. Take care that you do not accidentally cut your work!

When sewing in yarn tails, use a blunt tapestry needle with a large eye. A blunt needle will help prevent working between the fibres of the yarn.

Stitch markers are useful for a number of reasons. They can be used to mark the start of a round or to mark the start of individual repeats within a round. Not only can they save you a lot of counting, but they can also save you

ripping out a lot of stitches (known as frogging). If you do not have stitch markers, use a piece of scrap yarn to mark your stitches instead.

When sewing motifs together, you might find it useful to use pins to keep the motifs together while you work. Use rust-proof pins with large heads.

HOOK SIZES

All of the projects in this book use hooks smaller than 10 mm (US N/P/15). Hook sizes are specified at the start of each pattern.

GAUGE/TENSION

For many of the projects in this book, tension is not important. Some projects will need to be made with a tight tension, such as cushions to be stuffed, while other projects, like garments, will need to be made to an exact tension. In these cases, it's important that you work up a tension swatch first to check the appearance, density, and size of your work.

If you find that using the specified hook for any particular pattern makes your work too loose or lacy, try going down a hook size. If your work is too tight or dense, try going up a hook size.

ABBREVIATIONS

The patterns in this book feature a number of standard terms and abbreviations which are listed below.

beg	beginning
BLO	back loop only
BP	back post
CC	contrasting colour
ch	chain
cl	cluster
dc	double crochet
dc2tog	double crochet next 2sts together
dtr2tog	double treble next 2sts together
FLO	front loop only
FP	front post
MC	main colour
patt	pattern
pc	popcorn
rep	repeat
RS	right side
sl st	slip stitch
sp(s)	spaces
st(s)	stitches
tch	turning chain
tr	treble crochet
tr2tog	treble crochet next 2sts together
WS	wrong side
yoh	yarn over hook
yoke	the shaped area of the neckline and shoulders in a garment

Starting to Crochet

HOLDING YOUR HOOK

People generally hold their hook in one of two ways, the knife hold or the pencil hold. You can use whichever method you find most comfortable. You should hold your hook in your dominant hand while the non dominant hand holds the yarn and controls the tension of your yarn.

Knife Hold

Hold your hook as you would hold your knife when you are eating. Most hooks have a flat surface called a thumb rest; the tip of your thumb should be pressed flat against the thumb rest.

Pencil Hold

Hold your hook as if you are holding a pencil. Your thumb sits on the thumb rest, and the tip of your forefinger supports the back of the hook.

HOLDING YOUR YARN

There are lots of different ways to hold your yarn. Below are the two main options, woven and forefinger.

Woven

Weave the yarn through your fingers as shown: over your index finger, under your middle finger, and over your ring finger. If this feels too loose, wrap the yarn around your little finger once, like a ring.

Forefinger

Wrap the yarn around your forefinger twice.

SLIP KNOT

Place the end of the yarn in your left palm (right if you are left handed) and hold it in place with your pinkie and ring finger. Wrap the yarn clockwise around your forefinger so that the working yarn crosses over the tail of yarn and forms a loop. Insert your hook into the loop, catch the working tail of yarn with your hook, and pull it through the loop. Hold both ends of yarn and pull them tight, but not too tight, until the slip knot rests against your hook.

CHAIN STITCH AND FOUNDATION CHAIN

1. With a slip knot on your hook, hold the non working end of the yarn between your thumb and middle finger. Swing your hook from front to back UNDER the working yarn so that the working yarn forms a 'loop' over your hook. This is known as a yarn over hook. Still holding the non working end, pull it slightly away from the hook.

2. Pull the loop created by the yarn over through the loop that is already on your hook. Make sure that the hook is pointing downward, otherwise it will catch on the loop that is already on your hook. You have now made your first chain stitch.

TURNING CHAINS

Turning chains are used to bring the start of a row/round up to the necessary height so that the top of the turning chain is in line with the tops of the rest of the stitches. The turning chain usually replaces the first stitch, but not always. Slip stitches do not require a turning chain. Double crochet stitches require one turning chain, but it is not counted as a stitch. Half double crochet stitches require two turning chains; this 2ch is counted as your first stitch. Double treble crochet stitches require three turning chains; this 3ch is counted as as your first stitch. Treble crochet requires four turning chains; this 4ch is counted as your first stitch. Please note that there are always exceptions to these general rules so read the individual pattern carefully.

Basic Stitches

SLIP STITCH (SL ST)

Slip stitches do not add any height to your work. They are usually used to join rounds. They can also be used to join separate pieces of fabric together or to reinforce an edge.

To make a slip stitch into the foundation chain, insert your hook into top loop only of the second chain from the hook. Wrap the yarn over the hook and pull through both loops on your hook.

To make a slip stitch in subsequent rows/rounds, insert your hook into both loops of the indicated stitch. Yarn over and pull through both loops on your hook.

DOUBLE CROCHET (DC)

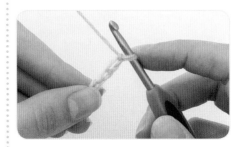

1. Insert your hook into the top loop only of the second chain from the hook.

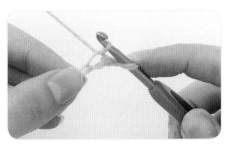

2. Yarn over hook by swinging your hook front to back UNDER the working yarn. Pull up a loop. You will now have 2 loops on your hook.

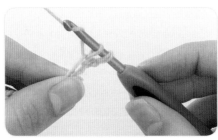

3. Pull through both loops on your hook to complete the first double crochet. Insert your hook into the next stitch and repeat Steps 2 and 3. Repeat until you have worked into every chain stitch in the foundation chain.

4. For the next row, make one (turning) chain, then turn your work. Insert your hook under both loops of the first stitch and repeat Steps 2 and 3. Repeat for each stitch across. Your last double crochet should sit in the first double crochet of the previous round. Do not work into the turning chain.

HALF TREBLE CROCHET (HTR)

1. Yarn over hook and insert your hook into the top loop only of the third chain from the hook.

2. Yarn over hook again and pull up a loop. There should now be 3 loops on your hook.

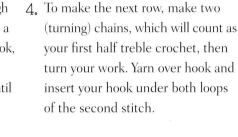

3. Yarn over hook again and pull through all 3 loops on your hook to complete a first half treble crochet. Yarn over hook, insert the hook into the next stitch, and repeat Steps 2 and 3. Repeat until you have worked into every chain stitch in the foundation chain.

4. To make the next row, make two (turning) chains, which will count as your first half treble crochet, then turn your work. Yarn over hook and insert your hook under both loops of the second stitch.

5. Complete Steps 2 and 3. Repeat for each stitch across the row. Your last half treble crochet should fall in the second chain of the turning 2ch at the start of the previous row.

PLEASE NOTE

Occasionally a designer won't count this turning 2ch as a stitch. In that case, you will make your first stitch in the top loop of the first stitch, and your last stitch will fall in the last half treble crochet, not in the top of the turning 2ch. To avoid confusion, follow the pattern instructions meticulously and count your stitches at the end of each row/round.

TREBLE CROCHET (TR)

1. Yarn over hook and insert your hook into the top loop only of the fourth chain from the hook.

2. Yarn over hook again and pull up a loop. There should now be 3 loops on your hook.

3. Yarn over hook again and pull through 2 loops. There should now be 2 loops on your hook.

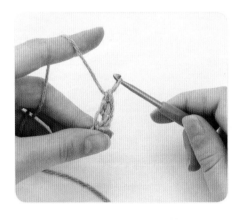

4. Yarn over hook and pull through both remaining loops on your hook to complete your first treble crochet. Yarn over hook, insert your hook into the next stitch, and repeat Steps 2 to 4. Repeat into every chain stitch in the foundation chain.

5. To make the next row, make three (turning) chains, which will count as your first double crochet, then turn your work.

6. Yarn over hook and insert your hook under both loops of the second stitch. Complete steps 2 to 4.

DOUBLE TREBLE CROCHET (DTR)

1. Yarn over hook twice and insert your hook into the top loop only of the fifth chain from the hook.

2. Yarn over hook again and pull up a loop. There should now be 4 loops on your hook.

3. (Yarn over hook and pull through 2 loops) three times to complete your first double treble crochet.

4. To make the next double treble crochet, yarn over hook twice, insert your hook into the next stitch, and repeat Steps 2 to 3. Repeat until you have worked into every chain stitch in the foundation chain.

5. To make the next row, make four (turning) chains, which will count as your first treble crochet, and turn your work. Yarn over hook twice and insert your hook under both loops of the second stitch. Complete steps 2 to 3. Repeat for each stitch across. Your last double treble crochet should sit in the fourth chain of the turning 4ch at the start of the previous row.

Increasing and Decreasing

INCREASING

Whether you are using double, half treble, treble, or double treble crochet, the method remains the same.

To increase by one stitch at the beginning, middle, or end of a row/round, simply make 2 stitches in the same stitch.

DECREASING

Double Crochet Decrease (dc2tog)

1. Insert your hook through both loops of the indicated stitch and pull up a loop. Insert your hook into the next stitch and pull up a loop. There should now be 3 loops on your hook.

2. Yarn over hook and pull through all 3 loops.

Half Treble Crochet Decrease (htr2tog)

1. Yarn over hook and insert your hook through both loops of the indicated stitch. Yarn over hook and pull up a loop. Yarn over hook and insert your hook into the next stitch. Yarn over hook and pull up a loop. There should now be 5 loops on your hook.

2. Yarn over hook and pull through all 5 loops.

Treble Crochet Decrease (tr2tog)

1. Yarn over hook and insert your hook through both loops of the indicated stitch. Yarn over hook and pull up a loop. Yarn over hook and pull through 2 loops. There should now be 2 loops on your hook. Yarn over hook and insert your hook into the next stitch. Yarn over hook and pull up a loop. Yarn over hook and pull through 2 loops on your hook. There should now be 3 loops on your hook.

2. Yarn over hook and pull through all 3 loops. Occasionally you will need to make a tr2tog at the very start of a row/round. In these instances you will work 2ch and tr in the next st. This will count as your Beginning Treble Crochet Decrease (Beg Tr2tog).

Special Stitches

POST STITCHES

Front Post Stitches

Identify the post of the stitch you want to work around. Insert your hook from the front to the back and then from the back to the front around the post so that the post lies on top of your hook. Complete your stitch as normal.

Back Post Stitches

Back post stitches are a bit trickier than front post stitches, but once you get the hang of them you will love them!

1. Identify the post of the stitch you want to work around. Insert your hook from the back to the front and then from the front to the back around the post so that the post lies behind your hook.

2. Complete your stitch as normal. You might find it easier to twist your work forward to see what you are doing.

Loop Stitch

The loop stitch is a variation of double crochet that creates loops on the wrong side of your work.

1. Hold your work as you normally would, with your hook in the one hand and your other hand supporting both your work and yarn. Insert your hook into the next stitch.

2. Form a loop of yarn around the index finger of your non hook hand.

3. Pass the hook behind both strands of this loop and catch the far side of the loop.

4. Pull this side through your stitch as you normally would when pulling up a loop, being careful to keep the loop around your index finger. You should have 2 loops on your hook.

5. Yarn over hook and pull through both loops to complete the stitch.

6. Repeat this for every loop stitch.

FRONT LOOP ONLY STITCHES (FLO)

Just like with chain stitches, the top of each double crochet, half treble crochet, treble crochet, and double treble crochet forms a 'V'.

Front loop only stitches are made by inserting your hook into the front loop only, not through both loops. The front loop will always be the one closest to you when you are holding your work.

BACK LOOP ONLY STITCHES (BLO)

Back loop only stitches are made by inserting your hook into the back loop only, not through both loops. The back loop will always be the one farthest away from you when you are holding your work.

STANDING DC

1. Start by making a slip knot on your hook with the new yarn.

4. Pull up a loop.

2. Insert your hook into the indicated stitch or space.

3. Yarn over the hook.

5. Yarn over the hook again.

6. Pull through both loops on the hook.

PLEASE NOTE

To make a standing htr, wrap the yarn around the hook once and then simply follow the instructions for standing tr, but at step 4, pull through the first three loops on the hook. Once you are left with one loop on the hook, your standing htr is complete and you can continue with the pattern.

STANDING TR

1. Wrap the yarn around the hook twice.

2. Insert your hook into the indicated stitch or space. Yarn over the hook.
3. Pull up a loop.
4. Yarn over hook and pull through the first two loops on the hook.

5. Yarn over hook and pull through the remaining two loops on the hook.

SPIKE STITCH

1. Insert the hook through the designated stitch two or more rows below. The number of rows down will determine how long the spike stitch is.

2. Draw the yarn through the stitch and back up to the working level.

3. Yarn over hook (yoh) and draw the yarn through the 2 loops on your hook.

4. Continue to work until you are ready to add another spike stitch.

Working in the Round

When you work in the round, there are three methods with which to start. These are interchangeable, so use whichever method you prefer. When substituting methods, make sure that your stitch count is correct at the end of the first round.

MAKING YOUR FIRST ROUND INTO ONE CHAIN

This is the easiest of the 3 methods. You will need to start with a turning chain + 1. For example, if your first round is treble crochet, you will need 4 chains (turning chain of 3 + 1 extra). The turning chain will count as your first stitch. The extra stitch will be your centre and all the other stitches for the round will be made into it.

For example, work 4ch. Make 11 treble crochet stitches into the fourth chain from the hook. This will give you a stitch count of 12 for your first round.

'RING OF CHAINS'

This method works well if your first round has a lot of stitches because you can make a bigger 'Ring of Chains' to accommodate them without bunching or overlapping. This method does leave a hole in the middle of your work, though, so if you want a tight centre, use one of the other two methods.

You will need to start with a short chain. Join this chain into a ring by making a slip stitch into the chain farthest away from your hook. Make the required turning chain and then work the remainder of the round into this ring.

For example, work 6ch. Join to the first chain with a sl st to form a ring. 3ch (this counts as your first treble crochet). Make 11 treble crochet stitches into the ring. This gives you a stitch count of 12 for your first round.

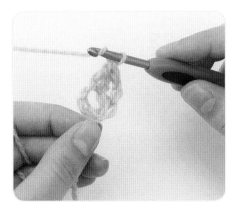

TIP

When using this method, work over your initial tail of yarn as you go. You can then pull on this tail of yarn once the round is complete to close the central hole. Make sure that you work this tail in securely to prevent the center from opening up again.

MAGIC RING

The magic ring is the trickiest of the three methods, but it is the most versatile. It can either yield a completely closed center, or accommodate as many stitches as you need.

For example, 3ch (this counts as your first treble crochet). Make 11 treble crochet stitches into the magic ring. This will give you a stitch count of 12 for your first round.

When using this method, it is extremely important that you work your initial tail of yarn away very securely. If it comes undone, your whole project might unravel.

1. Place the end of the yarn in your left palm (right if you are left handed) and hold it in place with your pinkie and ring finger. Wrap the yarn clockwise around your forefinger so that the working yarn crosses over the tail of yarn and forms a loop.

2. Remove the loop from your finger and hold it by pinching the point where the two strands of yarn overlap.

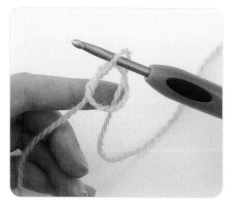

3. Insert your hook into the loop, catch the working tail of yarn with your hook, and pull it through the loop.

4. Yarn over and make a chain stitch to secure your working yarn. Make the required turning chain and work the remainder of the round into the magic ring. Remember to work over the initial tail of yarn as well. Close the hole by pulling on the initial tail of yarn.

INVISIBLE JOIN

1. Once you have made all the required stitches for the round, break off your yarn, leaving about a 10 cm (4 in) tail, and pull this tail all the way through the top of the last stitch made. Now pick up your tapestry needle and thread it with the tail of yarn. Insert your needle under both loops of the second stitch of the round. Pull the yarn tight, but not too tight.

2. Insert your needle into the top of the last stitch made. You want to insert it straight down into the eye formed by the loops. Make sure that you insert your needle through the third loop behind the stitch as well.

JOINING WITH A SLIP STITCH

1. Insert your hook into the first stitch of the round, remembering that the turning chain counts as a stitch.

2. Yarn over hook and pull through both the stitch and the loop on your hook to create a sl st. Sew in your tails of yarn.

3. Pull your yarn through. This will form a 'false' stitch. Make sure that you don't pull it too tight. You want this 'false' stitch to be more or less the same size as your other stitches. To secure this stitch, insert your needle from top to bottom into the third loop behind the stitch and pull the yarn through again. Now sew in your tails of yarn (see Sewing in Tails).

Changing Colours

You can use this method to join your new colour (or a new ball of yarn) at the beginning or the middle of a row/round.

1. You will need to change your colour on the last yarn over hook of the last stitch before the colour change. In other words, stop when you have 2 loops left on your hook.

2. Let go of the old colour and pick up the new colour. Draw the new colour through both loops to complete the stitch and continue as normal.

Finishing Your Work

BREAKING OFF

After making your last stitch, cut the yarn about 10 cm (4 in) away from your work.

1. Pull on your hook to create a large loop and then remove your hook. Thread the tail of yarn through this loop.

2. Pull the yarn tight to fasten off. It will create a knot. Work away your tails of yarn (see Sewing in Tails).

SEWING IN TAILS

A pattern will usually tell you to work away your 'loose ends' or tails of yarn at the end. To do that, you need a blunt tapestry needle and a pair of scissors.

Thread the tapestry needle with the tail of yarn. Working on the wrong side of the fabric, thread your needle through at least 5 cm (2 in) of stitches. Pull the yarn through all the way. Working in the opposite direction, and missing the first stitch, insert your needle back into the same stitches again. Missing the first stitch is essential, because it gives the yarn something to grip on to. Pull the yarn through again. Cut the yarn close to your work, being careful not to cut one of your stitches. If you have done this neatly, your tails won't be visible on the front of your work.

BLOCKING

Sometimes projects require blocking. This makes sewing individual pieces together easier, and creates a neat finish. You can either wet block or steam block.

Wet blocking

This method is suitable for all types of yarn. Pin the piece to the correct size (with the right side facing up), or pin it out so that it is tight but not too stretched. Using a spray bottle, mist the piece with cold water until it is damp but not wet. Allow the pieces to dry completely before removing the pins.

Steam blocking

Steam blocking is best suited to natural fibres like wool and cotton, as it is easy to accidentally melt your work if you are using synthetic fibres like acrylic. Pin the piece out on your ironing board, making sure that it is tight but not stretched out, and put your iron on the steam setting. Keep the iron about an inch above your work and blast it with steam, so that the steam penetrates the fibres without the iron touching the yarn. Leave to dry for at least 30 minutes and remove the pins.

SEAMS, JOINING, AND DETAIL

Whip Stitch

This stitch works really well on straight edges, such as when sewing the panels of a bag or cushion together.

With the right sides of the fabric pieces held together, insert the tapestry needle from the front to the back of a stitch and through the corresponding stitch on the other piece. Bring the needle to the front again and repeat until the seam is finished.

Running Stitch

Running stitch is used to attach appliqué pieces to your work and has a decorative dotted line appearance.

With the right side of your work facing you, insert your yarn needle from front to back into the indicated stitch and pull through. Insert your needle from back to front into the next stitch and pull through. Continue in this way until you have attached the required piece of appliqué.

AFTERCARE

Now that you have made your projects, it is important to care for them correctly.

If you have used acrylic yarn, caring for your pieces is fairly straightforward. You can wash them in the washing machine and dry them as you would any other easy care garment. You might find that your pieces start pilling after a couple of uses/washes. This is easily remedied by running a dry shaving razor over the surface to get rid of any pilling. Please be gentle if you decide to do this, as you just want to remove pilling, not shave the actual yarn. Do not iron your pieces as this will 'kill' (melt) the yarn.

If you have used plant fibres, such as cotton or linen, wash and dry as you would any garment. You can also iron your pieces if you wish, too.

If you have used animal fibres, such as wool, wash your items by hand and roll them in a towel to remove most of the moisture. Then lay them out flat to dry, shaping them as required. If you notice any pilling, gently scrape a dry razor over the surface to remove the pilling. Woollen items tend to pill less over time, unlike acrylic items which will keep on pilling.

Index

Yarns Used in the Projects

Rainbow Band Booties

Scheepjes Merino Soft; 50% Wool/ 25% Acrylic/25% Microfibre, 50 g (1.76 oz), 105 m (115 yd).
* 1 ball in C1 606 Da Vinci. Small amounts in each of the following colours: C2 615 Soutine, C3 646 Miro, C4 621 Picasso, C5 644 Duerer, C6 635 Matisse.

Gumdrops Pullover

Cascade Avalon; 50% Cotton/ 50% Acrylic, 100 g (3.5 oz), 160 m (175 yd).
* 2 [2, 2] balls in A 20 Heather. Small amounts in each of the following colours: B 14 Golf Green, C 09 Bird of Paradise, D 18 Turkish Sea, E 10 Artisan's Gold, F 27 Raspberry.

Ombré Socks

Debbie Bliss Baby Cashmerino; 55% Wool/33% Acrylic/12% Cashmere, 50 g (1.75 oz), 125 m (137 yd).
* 1 ball in each of the following colours:
Blue socks
A 100 White, B 204 Baby blue, C 071 Pool, D 059 Mallard.
Yellow socks
A 100 White, B 001 Primrose, C 091 Acid Yellow, D 083 Butter.

Little Flowers Playsuit

Drops Alpaca Silk Bushed; 100% Alpaca, 50 g (1.8 oz), 167 m (183 yd).
* 1 [2] balls in 100 Off White. Small amounts in each of the following colours:

Rainbow Striped Cardigan

Scheepjes Softfun; 60% Cotton/ 40% Acrylic, 50 g (1.76 oz), 140 m (153 yd).
* 3 balls in MC 2412. 1 ball in each of the following colours: CC1 2410, CC2 2518, CC3 2517, CC4 2452, CC5 2463.

Rainbow Striped Sun Hat

Scheepjes Softfun; 60% Cotton/ 40% Acrylic, 50 g (1.76 oz), 140 m (153 yd).
* 2 balls in MC 2412. Small amounts in each of the following colours: CC1 2410, CC2 2518, CC3 2517, CC4 2452, CC5 2463.

Citrus Nappy Cover

Scheepjes Softfun; 60% Cotton/ 40% Acrylic, 50 g (1.76 oz), 140 m (153 yd).
* 1 ball in each of the following colours: A 2518, B 2412, C 2410, D 2427, E 2517.

Snuggly Monster Mitts

Scheepjes Softfun; 60% Cotton/ 40% Acrylic, 50 g (1.76 oz), 140 m (153 yd).
* 1 ball in MC 2412. Small amounts in each of the following colours: CC1 2410, CC2 2518, CC3 2517, CC4 2452, CC5 2463.

Spring Stripes Dress

Scheepjes Catona; 100% Cotton, 63 m (69 yd), 25 g (0.88 oz).
* 3 [4] balls in A 100 Lemon Chiffon. B 256 Cornelia Rose, C 222 Tulip, D 385 Crystalline.

Spring Stripes Leggings

Scheepjes Catona; 100% Cotton, 63 m (69 yd), 25 g (0.88 oz).
* 2 balls in A 100 Lemon Chiffon. B 256 Cornelia Rose, C 222 Tulip, D 385 Crystalline.

Walk in the Park Hoodie

Lion Brand Vanna's Choice Baby; 100% acrylic, 155 m (170 yd), 100 g (3.5 oz).
* 2 balls in A 108 Bluebell. 1 ball in B 139 Berrylicious. Small amount in C 157 Duckie.

Hot Air Balloon Bunting

Scheepjes Catona; 100% Cotton, 63 m (69 yd), 25 g (0.88 oz).
* 1 ball in each of the following colours: A 258 Rosewood, B 208 Yellow Gold,
* C 391 Deep Ocean Great, D 282 Ultra Violet, E 173 Bluebell, F 205 Kiwi.

Little Bear Rattle

Scheepjes Catona; 100% Cotton, 63 m (69 yd), 25 g (0.88 oz).
* 1 ball in each of the following colours: A 179 Topaz, B 146 Vivid Blue, C 397 Cyan, D 280 Lemon, E 281 Tangerine, F 256 Cornelia Rose.

Friendly Soft Toys

Scheepjes Stone Washed; 78% cotton/ 22% acrylic, 130 m (142 yd), 50 g (1.75 oz).
Bunny
* 2 balls in A 818 Lilac Quartz. 1 ball in each of the following colours: B 821 Pink Quartzite, F 811 Deep Amethyst. Small amount in C 813 Amazonite, D 820 Rose Quartz, E 819 New Jade.
Dog
* 2 balls in E 819 New Jade. 1 ball in D 820 Rose Quartz. Small amounts in each of the following colours: A 818 Lilac Quartz, C 813 Amazonite, D 820 Rose Quartz, F 811 Deep Amethyst.

Textured Stacking Blocks

Scheepjes Softfun; 60% Cotton/ 40% Acrylic, 140 m (153 yd), 50 g (1.75 oz).
* 1 ball in each of the following colours: A 2410, B 2511, C 2427, D 2516, E 2495, F 2518, G 2532.

Sunny Day Headband

Scheepjes Catona; 100% Cotton, 63 m (69 yd), 25 g (0.88 oz).

* 1 ball in A 130. Small amounts in each of following colours: B 115, C 280, D 205, E 400.
* Cloud: Small amount of F 173.
* Sun: Small amount of G 208.

Pastel Chevron Hat

Scheepjes Softfun Denim; 60% cotton/40% acrylic, 140 m (153 yd), 50 g (1.75 oz).
* 1 ball in A 2412. Small amounts of each of the following colours: B 504, C 512, D 509, E 516, F 518.

Pastel Chevron Mittens

Scheepjes Softfun Denim; 60% cotton/40% acrylic, 140 m (153 yd), 50 g (1.75 oz).
* 1 ball in A 2412. Small amounts in each of the following colours: B 504, C 512, D 509, E 516, F 518.

Gradient Floor Blanket

Cascade 220 Superwash; 100% Wool, 200 m (220 yd), 100 g (3.5 oz).
* 4 balls in A 871 White. 1 ball in each of the following colours : B 809 Really Red, C 825 Orange, D 821 Daffodil, E 820 Lemon, F 851 Lime, G 850 Lime Sherbert, H 848 Blueberry, I 844 Periwinkle, J 837 Berry Pink, K 835 Pink Rose, L 837 Very Berry, M 1973 Seafoam Heather, N 1969 Heather.

Pretty Mary Janes

Drops Paris; 100% cotton, 75 m (82 yd), 50 g (1.75 oz).
* 1 ball in each of the following colours: A 17 Off White, B 31 Medium Purple.
* Small amounts in each of the following colours: E 19 Light Yellow, F 01 Apricot.
Drops Cotton Light; 50% Cotton/50% Polyester, 105 m (115 yd), 50 g (1.8 oz).
* Small amounts in each of the following colours: C 08 Ice Blue, D 11 Green.

Bobble Pacifier Cords

Cascade 220 Superwash; 100% Wool, 200 m (220 yd), 100 g (3.5 oz).
* 1 ball in MC 871 White.
* Small amount in one of the following colours : 825 Orange, 820 Lemon, 851 Lime, 837 Berry Pink, 1973 Seafoam Heather, 1969 Heather.

Whatever the Weather Wall Hanging

Bernat Super Value; 100% Acrylic, 389 m (425 yd), 197 g (7 oz).
* Small amounts in each of the following colours: A 445 White, B 615 Yellow, C 615 Carrot, D 610 Royal Blue, E 246 Lush, F 517 True Red, G 520 Cool Blue.
Cascade 220 Solid; 100% Wool, 200 m (220 yd), 100 g (3.5 oz).
* Small amount in H 7827 Goldenrod.

Climbing Colours Blanket

Red Heart Baby Hugs Medium; 100% Acrylic, 225 m (247 yd), 127 g (4.5 oz).
* 4 balls in 4001 A Frosting. 1 ball in each of the following colours: B 4909 Ladybug, C 4255 Orangie, D 4201 Sunny, E 4562 Aloe, F 4825 Bluie, G 4538 Lilac.

Mini Nesting Baskets

Scheepjes Stone Washed XL; 70% Cotton/30% Acrylic, 75 m (82 yd), 50 g (1.76 oz).
* 1 ball in each of the following colours: 847 Red Jasper, 856 Coral, 852 Lemon Quartz, 853 Amazonite.

Freddie Frog Bottle Cosy

Scheepjes Softfun; 60% Cotton/40% Acrylic, 140 m (153 yd), 50 g (1.76 oz).
* 1 ball in each of the following colours: A 2432, B 2519. Small amounts in each of the following colours: C 2516, D 2517, E 2518, F 2480, G 2412, H 2532.

Monster Cushion Cover

Scheepjes Stone Washed XL; 70% Cotton/30% Acrylic, 75 m (82 yd), 50g (1.76 oz).
* 2 balls in A 853 Amazonite. 1 ball in each of the following colours: B 846 Canada Jade, C 856 Coral, D 857 Citrine, E 841 Moon Stone.

Fun Shapes Organiser

Scheepjes Bloom; 100 Cotton, 80 m (87 yd), 50 g (1.76 oz).
* 4 balls in A 419 Forget-me-not. 1 ball in each of the following colours: B 413 Gerbera, C 408 Tiger Lily, D 406 Tulip, E 422 Old Lily, F 414 Sun Flower.

Drops Storage Basket

Scheepjes Roma Big; 132 m (144 yd), 220 g (7.76 oz).
* 3 balls in A 25. 1 ball in B 3.
Scheepjes Catona; 100% Cotton, 63 m (69 yd), 25 g (0.88 oz).
* Small amounts in each of the following colours: C 258 Rosewood, D 208 Yellow Gold, E 205 Kiwi, F 391 Deep Ocean Great, G 282 Ultra Violet.

Rainbow Waves Buggy Blanket

Scheepjes Merino Soft; 50% Wool/25% Acrylic/25% Microfibre, 105 m (115 yd), 50 g (1.76 oz).
* 2 balls in G 640 Warhol, H 645 van Eyck. 1 ball in each of the following colours: A 638 Hockney, B 602 Raphael, C 621 Picasso, D 614 Magritte, E 646 Miro, F 615 Soutine.

Buddy Bear Curtain Tie

Drops Cotton Light; 50% Cotton/50% Polyester, 105 m (115 yd), 50 g (1.75 oz).
* 1 ball in each of the following colours: A 25 Light Lilac, B 23 Light Purple, C 18 Pink, D 05 Light Pink, E 01 Off White.
Drops Love You 5; 100% Cotton, 75 m (115 yd), 50 g (1.75 oz). F 117 Purple.

Meet the Designers

KIRSTEN BALLERING

Ombré Socks 15 ∘ Gradient Floor Blanket 62 ∘ Bobble Pacifier Cords 69
Kirsten discovered crochet while living in Sweden and hasn't stopped creating since! She's passionate about designing colourful and functional projects and works from her studio in the Netherlands, where she lives together with her fiancé and cats. You'll never find her hands idle! Follow her blog on haakmaarraak.nl.

CAROLYN CHRISTMAS

Stacking Blocks 50 ∘ Freddie Frog Bottle Cosy 78 ∘ Fun Shapes Organiser 87
Carolyn started designing years ago after giving birth to twins. In the ensuing years, she has been a crochet designer, magazine and book editor, teacher, author and publisher. Nowadays, she and her husband, David, live and work in their 100-year-old home in the Texas Hill Country. You can find Carolyn's designs at pinkmambo.com.

SOPHIE CORMIER

Little Flowers Playsuit 19 ∘ Whatever the Weather Wall Hanging 72
Sophie has been crocheting and designing for four years and knitting for seven. She lives on the beautiful east coast of Canada with her two children. Owner of *Illumikniti Designs* and a self-proclaimed yarn hoarder, she knits beautiful props for photographers. You can find her work and patterns at newbornprops.ca.

SHELLEY HUSBAND

Sunny Day Headband 55
Shelley is a long-time crafter whose current passion is designing crochet patterns. Her patterns gently encourage crocheters to extend their skills to create items they didn't think themselves able to do. She lives with her husband and teenage daughters in a tiny town on the coast of Victoria, Australia. Find all her patterns and tutorials on spincushions.com.

CARMEN JORISSEN

Little Bear Rattle 44 ∘ Friendly Soft Toys 47
Carmen is a designer specialising in cute amigurumi toys and quirky home decor items. She started her creative blog back in 2012 and in 2014 she was awarded the *Mollie Makes Youth Award*. Browse through her colourful Instagram feed at @crafty_queens and find free patterns on craftyqueens.nl.

DOROTEJA KARDUM

Rainbow Band Booties 8 ∘ Pretty Mary Janes 66 ∘ Buddy Bear Curtain Tie 96
Doroteja Kardum is the blogger and crochet designer behind *Croby Pattern Designs*. After learning to crochet a few years ago, it has since become the source of a lifestyle full of creativity and happiness. Doroteja's favourite things to crochet are baby clothes, shoes and toys. You can find her creations on crobypatterns.com.

TATSIANA KUPRYIANCHYK

Rainbow Waves Pram Blanket 93 ∘ Monster Cushion Cover 84
Tatsiana Kupryianchyk is a designer and the creative mind behind *Lilla Björn Crochet*. As well as focusing on home accessories and soft toys, Tatsiana is obsessed with mandala art, which allows her to spend long hours playing with yarns and learning new techniques. Find Tatsiana's designs at http://www.lillabjorncrochet.com and on Instagram at @lillabjorncrochet.

RHONDDA MOL

Rainbow Striped Cardigan 21 ∘
Rainbow Striped Sun Hat 25 ∘
Snuggly Monster Mitts 30 ∘
Pastel Chevron Hat 57 ∘ Pastel
Chevron Mittens 60

Rhondda is a freelance Crochet
Designer and a full-time Blogger at
Oombawka Design Crochet. Here she
shares her love of crochet with the
online crochet community through
her beginner friendly free patterns
and tutorials. She currently resides in
Ontario, Canada with her husband
and two young children. Find her
patterns on Ravelry as RhonddaM
and follow her daily crochet blog at
oombawkadesigncrochet.com.

AMY RAMNARINE

Citrus Nappy Cover 27 ∘ Spring
Stripes Dress 32 ∘ Spring Stripes
Leggings 34 ∘ Whatever the Weather
Wall Hanging 72

Amy has been designing her own
crochet patterns professionally since
2012. Her creations are all made at
her home in New York, where she lives
with her husband, son and daughter.
Amy loves to crochet, craft and create
recipes. She shares her crochet
creations and crafting adventures on
her blog: thestitchinmommy.com.

PIA THADANI

Gumdrops Pullover 10 ∘
Walk in the Park Hoodie 36 ∘
Climbing Colours Blanket 76

Pia is the designer and blogger behind
StitchesNScraps.com. She is also
a member of the Crochet Guild of
America and has earned the Master
of Advanced Crochet Stitches &
Techniques designation. She loves
variety, so she enjoys creating different
kinds of designs and exploring new
techniques and stitch combinations.

DEDRI UYS

Hot Air Balloon Bunting 42 ∘
Mini Nesting Baskets 78 ∘
Drops Storage Basket 90

Dedri Uys is the author of *Big Hook
Rag Crochet* and *Amamani Puzzle
Balls*. Dedri is passionate about
crochet and shares her love of the
craft through online patterns and
tutorials. She lives in London with
her husband, three sons and the family
cat. Find her patterns on Ravelry
at dedri-uys or follow her blog at
lookatwhatimade.net.

Acknowledgements

The publisher would like to thank the following for their help in making this book:

Dedri Uys, for her fantastic eye for design, crocheting expertise and curatorial skills which brought the designers together.

Thank you to the wonderful crocheters for designing and making the projects: Kirsten Ballering, Carolyn Christmas, Sophie Cormier, Shelley Husband, Carmen Jorissen, Doroteja Kardum, Tatsiana Kupryianchyk, Rhondda Mol, Amy Ramnarine and Pia Thadani.

Many thanks to Scheepjeswol (www.scheepjes.com) for supplying the beautiful yarn for many of the projects.

Thank you to photographer Simon Pask, and our models Beau Raviraj, Sigraveana Connell, Gemma Hickingbotham, Maisen Hall, Martha Minter and Kayden Rajoo for bringing the projects to life.

Thanks also to Therese Chynoweth, Lindsay Kaubi, Jen Riley and Ann Barrett for their editorial work and index.

Rainbow Illustrations © NadineVeresk/Shutterstock.